OTHER BOOKS IN THIS SERIES

FRONTISPIECE

Softly molded, almost feminine lines of the 1961 250 short-wheelbase
berlinetta belie its fantastic performance. Pininfarina photo.

Dean Batchelor

Illustrated **FERRARI** BUYER'S GUIDE

Motorbooks International
Publishers & Wholesalers Inc.
Osceola, Wisconsin 54020, USA ®

© Dean Batchelor, 1981

ISBN: 0-87938-118-3
Library of Congress Catalog Card Number: 81-1256

Motorbooks International is a certified trademark,
registered with the United States Patent Office.

Printed and bound in the United States of America.
10 9 8 7 6 5 4

Cover illustration by David R. Faulkner, Los Angeles,
California.

Motorbooks International books are also available at
discounts in bulk quantity for industrial or
sales-promotion use. For details write to Marketing
Manager, Motorbooks International, P.O. Box 2, Osceola
Wisconsin 54020.

Sole distribution in the United Kingdom by
Motor Racing Publications Ltd.
28 Devonshire Road
London W4 2HD, England

Library of Congress Cataloging in Publication Data

Batchelor, Dean.
    Illustrated Ferrari buyer's guide.

    1. Ferrari automobile.   2. Automobiles—Purchasing.
I. Title.
TL215.F47B42   629.2'222   81-1256
ISBN 0-87938-118-3 (pbk.)   AACR2

CREDITS AND ACKNOWLEDGMENTS

I want to express my sincere and grateful thanks to those who contributed time, photos or information to aid the creation of this book.

Dean Batchelor

Karl Dedolph
Ed Niles
Bill Rudd
Pininfarina
Jonathan Thompson
Automotive Investment Newsletter, Vol. 1, No. 10—Stan Nowak
Ferrari Market Letter—Gerald Roush
Ferrari Cars 1962-1966—Brooklands Books
Ferrari Cars 1966-1969—Brooklands Books
Ferrari: The Sports & Gran Turismo Cars—Fitzgerald, Merritt & Thompson
Road & Track library
The Ferrari Legend: The Road Cars—Antoine Prunet
The Berlinetta Lusso—Kurt Miska
The Spyder California—George Carrick

TABLE OF CONTENTS

INTRODUCTION

So you think you want to own a Ferrari. Why? Or haven't you heard all the horror stories about the high cost of parts and service? And that the cars spend more time in the shop than they do on the road. And those Webers—how can you keep three carbs synchronized, let alone six on some models?

There are probably a hundred reasons why any intelligent person should not buy a Ferrari; but there is also a good reason why any car enthusiast should own one. It *is* a Ferrari, and there has been no car (Bugatti, Rolls-Royce, Alfa Romeo and Porsche notwithstanding) that has the mystique and charisma of a 12-cylinder Ferrari.

Assuming that you are, at least, considering the purchase of a Ferrari, and nothing can be done to talk you out of it, I'll do what I can to help you make a reasonable decision about which one to buy and, maybe, how much to spend.

The first thing you should do is learn as much as possible about Ferraris. This entails talking to knowledgeable enthusiasts and reading as much of the available literature as you can get your hands on.

Both approaches can present a problem if you don't have access to these information sources. Therefore, I have included a list of references at the end of the book.

Before going any further, I would like to strongly emphasize one point—researching information about Ferraris can be time-consuming and relatively expensive. If you can't afford the time and cost of research, you'd probably better reconsider buying a Ferrari (or any other exotic car, for that matter). It is, and will be, an expensive investment. The more you know, the safer your investment will be. It will be better by far to spend a few hundred dollars on books and magazines so you can buy the right Ferrari at the right price (or, decide to *not* buy a Ferrari), than to discover a mistake when it's too late.

Finding a Ferrari to buy can be done in a number of ways. Some of the best sources are the classified advertising sections of *Road & Track, Autoweek, Hemmings Motor News, Ferrari Market Letter, Old Cars* or in newspapers in large cities such as New York, Los Angeles, Chicago, San Francisco, Dallas, Detroit, Philadelphia, Boston, Atlanta or Miami. The newsletters published by the Ferrari clubs are also excellent.

Buying a car in Europe is a possibility, but isn't recommended for a number of reasons: 1) Most Ferraris came to the U.S. and are still here, somewhere; 2) Most late-model Ferraris still in Europe won't pass U.S. emission or safety standards and would require extensive (read *expensive*) modifications to be licensed here; 3) Most of the cost saving, if there is any, is lost in shipping and duty; 4) Many European car owners don't treat their cars as well as American car owners; 5) The dollar/mark, lira, schilling, pound exchange rate is unfavorable; and 6) Used car dealers are the same the world over, and the Europeans have been at it longer than their American counterparts (caveat emptor).

Most ads in the Ferrari club publications are pretty straightforward, because the seller knows he's reaching a reasonably knowledgeable potential buyer. The cars may or may not be *priced* right, but they should be pretty much as described.

This doesn't always hold true with newspaper or magazine ads. Witness the advertisements that make a point of saying "custom body by Farina" or "Borrani wire wheels" or "leather upholstery" or "Weber carburetors."

To the best of my knowledge, Ferrari has never built a body for one of his road cars. The bodies have *all* been built by Carrozzeria Touring, Pinin Farina (changed to Pininfarina in 1961), Allemano, Vignale, Boano, Ellena, Ghia, Ghia Aigle, Stabilimenti Farina, Bertone, Scaglietti or one of the smaller coachbuilders such as Fantuzzi, Neri & Bonacini, Drogo or Zagato.

Wheels were traditionally made by Borrani—first, bolt-on steel disc, then wire spoke with center-lock, knock-off hubs—until the GTB and GTS in the mid-sixties, which have Campagnolo alloy wheels (sometimes with Borrani wires as options). Later models have Cromadora alloy wheels.

I've also never heard of an original Ferrari with anything but leather or, in some cases, cloth upholstery. No Naugahydes or vinyls until the 246 GT.

And the vast majority of Ferraris have had Weber carburetors (the exceptions being a few cars with Solex carburetors, the racing cars with fuel injection and the 308 GTBi and 308 GTSi), particularly the Ferraris you're apt to find for sale.

So, finding an advertisement for a Ferrari with Borrani wire wheels, Weber carburetors and body by Pininfarina is no big deal as far as rarity is concerned.

If the car was built before 1955, or was built for sale in England, Australia, New Zealand or Japan, it could have either right- or left-hand drive. A few of the early cars had a reversed shift pattern and non-synchromesh transmissions were normal until the mid-fifties.

A factor to be considered by any buyer of an exoticar is whether he wants an *original* car for investment purposes, or a 'driver' which he can enjoy even if it isn't totally original.

This decision alone can make a tremendous difference in initial cost, and eventual maintenance. A substitute part that will work, but isn't original, can get your car back on the road quicker for less money; but may reduce the value to some extent. My suggestion, here, would be to keep the original part so that when you eventually sell the car you can offer the buyer all the original parts for the car—even if a part needs a complete rebuild. The new owner may want to restore the car to stock (original condition) and need that part.

This is particularly true of engine swaps. The cost of rebuilding a Ferrari engine or transmission has become so high that it may soon be common practice to install an American V-8 to replace the original V-12 when an overhaul is indicated.

Current rates in the better Ferrari shops run from thirty-five to fifty dollars per hour, depending on geographical location. Los Angeles and San Francisco are probably the highest. The labor rate, plus the ridiculously high cost of parts, can cause a normal V-12 ring-and-valve job to run as high as $6,000 (assuming a complication arises—which often happens), and a complete overhaul of a street V-12 can run $15,000. I've heard of a Ferrari V-12 competition engine overhaul topping $20,000, which included replacement of everything in the engine that moves—a total remanufacture.

With figures like these in mind, it's easy to see why there will be a substantial number of Ferrari engine swaps in the future.

Because of the high cost of an engine overhaul, it is essential that a good engine be your first priority when buying a used Ferrari. Paint, upholstery and body repair can be done by any competent craftsman, but an engine overhaul is something that should be done by an expert.

So how do you know whether or not the engine is good? You probably can't tell for certain, but there are some checks you can make that will help ease your mind.

Remove each breather cap (there is one on each side of the Ferrari V-12 engine) and shake it to see if water from condensation has accumulated. Then check the dipstick for oil level, and look for that grayish color that indicates water in the oil. At this time, also check the radiator cap to see if the water is clean, dirty or has evidence of oil.

Ask the owner to start the engine. A bit of exhaust smoke at this point is normal—a lot of smoke isn't. While the engine is idling, remove the radiator cap again. If there are bubbles it could indicate a blown head gasket or water pump seal.

When the engine water-temperature gauge reaches normal, the oil pressure at idle (around 850 rpm if everything is right) should read between twenty-five and fifty percent of the gauge's range. If pressure is near the fifty-percent-range area, chances are good that the engine is in pretty good shape.

Early 250 GT's, with inside plugs, have separate O-ring cylinder gaskets which tend to go bad. It is advisable to insist on a compression and leak-down percent check on any used car you buy, and particularly so on Ferrari 250 GT's. The inside-plug engines also had trays around the carburetors to catch fuel overflow which could start a fire if a loose plug wire caused arcing when a carburetor flooded. Make sure these trays are installed, and draining properly.

Next, ask the owner to drive the car while you observe from outside. Minor smoke from the pipes is acceptable, and fairly normal—particularly on older-model Ferraris. Heavy smoke on acceleration indicates worn valve guides, heavy smoke on deceleration means worn rings. If bad enough, either condition will call for cylinder head removal before too long.

Ferrari exhaust smoke is almost always caused by excessive wear of the valve guides and valve stems. Ferrari valve guide material is rather soft by American standards, and wear in this area will allow an excessive amount of oil to find its way into the combustion chambers and then into the exhaust system. I've heard that wear on rubbing engine parts increases by the square of the engine speed, so an engine that is run consistently at higher rpm will require new guides sooner than an engine that is run at slower speeds. Because the sound of a Ferrari V-12 is one of the great joys of Ferrari ownership, don't count on finding one which has never been driven in the high rpm range.

While observing the car from the outside, check to see if it tracks straight. If it 'crabtracks,' it likely means the car has been in an accident and wasn't properly repaired, or is in need of alignment in the later models with independent rear suspension.

A Ferrari V-12 engine is one of the smoothest running, and most responsive, engines ever installed in an automobile. If the idle is rough, it could be bad carburetor adjustment, or it could be worn carburetor linkage. The former isn't difficult to fix; the latter is, because it means replacement of the linkage, and possibly replacement of the carburetor bodies themselves.

Now it's time to drive the car. Because of the (probably) stiff clutch, and low inertia of the engine, it is difficult for the first-time Ferrari driver to move off smoothly. Practice will solve this problem.

A hissing noise from the clutch/transmission area might indicate worn shift forks, which is not a major problem. You can test for clutch slippage by quickly taking the car from stop up to about 6,000 rpm in third gear. If the clutch is weak, the engine will suddenly be over-revving for the indicated speed.

Once underway, watch the oil pressure gauge while cornering, particularly if driving vigorously. If pressure drops, chances are the oil pump pick-up hose is bad and needs replacing. Try downshifting without double-clutching. If it goes smoothly, the synchromesh rings are good. If downshifting can't be done smoothly, without a crunch, chances are pretty good that the transmission may need looking into (this is based on the assumption that the driver is somewhat competent—a ham-fisted driver won't complete a smooth, quiet shift with the best synchromesh in the world). And a Ferrari with rear-mounted transmission—275 GTB, 330 GTC, etc.—is difficult to shift from first to second when cold, even *with* a good transmission.

Unless you are determined, and very dedicated, try to buy a Colombo-engined Ferrari. The 'big-block' Lampredi V-12's have problem areas that are hard to deal with, now that parts are almost unobtainable.

On the Lampredi engines, the cylinders are screwed into the heads, eliminating head gasket problems, but the sealing rings at the bottom of the cylinders go bad from age, or just sitting around, and leak water into the oil. Also, if the timing chain is loose, it wears a hole in a water passage at the top of the timing gear case, letting water into the oil.

I strongly suggest that you buy a Pininfarina-bodied car if possible and, better yet, one that has lived in the southwestern part of the U.S. all its life. No evident rust prevention measures have been taken on some Scaglietti-bodied cars, and already rusted body panels have been seen to be installed on cars. The outside was, of course, cleaned and prepped for painting, but the inside was not de-rusted before assembly.

Okay, now that you have, or are about to get, your Ferrari, how do you take care of it so it will take care of you?

First, unless you plan to do all your own work (possible, but not necessarily recommended), you need a mechanic. He doesn't have to be a Ferrari specialist—although that is decidedly an advantage—but the key word here is *mechanic,* not a parts changer. Equipped with a full complement of metric tools, and a thorough working knowledge of carburetors, ignitions, suspension and steering, he'll be able to work on the Ferrari.

There are tricks and peculiarities of any car, but if the person is a real mechanic, he'll learn the tricks or know where to look to get answers. If he is merely a parts changer, you shouldn't let him near your Chevy or Ford, either. One of the best mechanics I found for my 250 GT was a Mercedes-Benz specialist, but he was an old-timer who understood engines and their various ancillary components.

I've owned three Ferraris, and not one of them required carburetion or ignition adjustments after they were set up (by Bill Rudd) correctly at the start. Two of the three (a 250 GT and a 340 Mexico) ran for three years without further adjustments.

11

My system was: a) don't tinker with the car myself (other than a straight-forward change of spark plugs or oil and filter), and b) warm up the *car* thoroughly before driving it hard.

The engine, transmission and driving axle assembly of any car is designed to operate best when the cases and internal moving parts are up to designated operating temperatures. This is especially critical for efficiency and longevity of cars with moving parts running in aluminum or magnesium cases.

Each morning (or after the car had not been run for several hours), after starting the engine, I ran it at a steady 1000 rpm for about a minute, then for maybe thirty seconds at 1500-2000 rpm. Revving a *cold* engine up and down from idle to 4000 or 5000 rpm may sound great, but does terrible things to stressed parts. You hear a lot of this at races, and the driver or mechanic doing it will tell you that he's ''keeping the plugs clean.'' This may be true, but he's also on an ego trip. Hopefully he's already warmed the engine so that parts are up to temperature.

Following the brief engine warm-up, I drove the first few miles at no more than 3000 rpm or thirty to thirty-five miles per hour until I felt both transmission and drive axle were also up to running temperature. The engine temperature gauge is a pretty good indication if the car is warmed up, because all three assemblies will reach optimum at about the same time.

Once these working parts are up to design temperatures, you can drive a Ferrari about as hard as you want to. It is rugged, durable and reliable—if you take care of it!

I don't know of a Ferrari that has failed its owner unless he's done something stupid with it. A Ferrari is a relatively complex vehicle, but it is not delicate or fragile. If you take care of it, you probably won't be let down. There will be exceptions, of course, but you could find those with any make of car.

Aside from the emotional aspect of owning and driving a Ferrari, the investment potential is probably the best you could find in a transportation device of any kind. The smallest increase in Ferrari values has been with the so-called production cars which have more than doubled their value in the past ten years. During the same period, any competition model has increased its value by eight to ten times, and some, even more. A 1963 250 GTO, which could have been purchased for $8,500 in 1971, will now bring upwards of $200,000. This appreciation ratio won't apply to other models of Ferrari, however. The GTO is a unique situation, not totally understood even by Ferrari fanatics.

Owning a Ferrari can be a tremendous emotional experience, either good or bad (sometimes both), depending on the owner's attitude and the particular vehicle's performance and reliability. It is the ultimate automotive hate/love affair; any auto enthusiast cannot be blamed for wanting to own at least one Ferrari.

INVESTMENT RATING

✿✿✿✿✿   The best. Highest prices, highest values, and best probability of further appreciation. You won't find these advertised in magazines or newspapers. They are sold like fine works of art or antiques—very occasionally at an auction, but most likely by word of mouth between knowledgeable collectors. Prices are well into six figures and climbing.

✿✿✿✿   Almost the best. Prices are in the high five-figure area. Like "the best," they will seldom, if ever, be offered in newspaper or magazine ads. If they are, they will probably be dogs, or, if any good at all, will be snapped up immediately. The investment potential is excellent because there will always be more potential buyers (when you want to re-sell) in this bracket, than there will be in the one above.

✿✿✿   Excellent value. These are desirable cars but the prices haven't gone berserk (as of this writing). Good combination of desirability and driveability. Expensive, but you wouldn't get apoplexy or hives worrying about it being parked in front of the restaurant while you're inside enjoying veal piccata and a bottle of soave.

✿✿   Good cars to drive and enjoy. All the great sounds of the Ferrari V-12, and they will do almost anything other Ferraris will do, but are not as exotic (they don't shout, 'hey look at me!'); and won't appreciate as much or as fast as cars in the first three categories.

✿   Any Ferrari that has had an engine swap and the original engine isn't available with the car, a car that has been in a bad accident, or a two-star-category car that needs total restoration.

The single most important factor in buying a used Ferrari is to find one with a good engine. In early 1981, you could still buy a Ferrari 250 2+2, or an early 250 GT, for about $10,000; but if the engine needed a substantial amount of work, you could end up with *another* $10,000 in an engine overhaul—and you'd still have a $10-15,000 car.

Following is a brief description of the Ferraris most likely to be found for sale. I have listed only 'street' or 'road' cars, as the probability of finding a racing car is negligible.

The years of manufacture are accurate; but in some cases the production run might begin in the early part of the year, and in others, later in the year. The serial number parameters (say, 0429-0921) indicate that all of the model series were built between those numbers, but not all cars built within the first and last numbers were of that model.

Following the model descriptions are: a list of authorized U.S. and Canadian Ferrari dealers, a list of Ferrari clubs, books about Ferraris, magazines that regularly cover Ferraris (and a list of previously-published articles about Ferraris) and source lists for cars, parts, service and accessories.

Manufacture was started in late 1954 on what is generally conceded to be the first production Ferrari. It was a second-series Europa, with the 2953 cc Colombo engine and 102.3-inch wheelbase, designated Europa GT. The first of this series had serial number 0357GT, and the last of the series was numbered 0427GT, built early in 1956.

These Ferraris were not production cars in the sense that we think of production today. But for a small, specialist car company it was a period of 'arrival' as a builder of touring cars. The chassis were as nearly alike as Ferrari could make them at the time, and most bodies were by Pinin Farina—again, nearly identical, although a few cars had Vignale bodywork.

Near the end of the model run, in late 1955, Pinin Farina began developing the lower hood and flattened-oval radiator opening that was to become the standard Ferrari shape for the coming years.

The Europa GT was the first Ferrari to use coil springs at the front. Previous models which were long wheelbase (110 inches) with Lampredi engines, had a single, transverse-leaf front spring. All had independent front suspension, however. Two semi-elliptic springs and a live axle at the rear, located by parallel trailing arms on each side, were continued from previous Ferrari designs.

Ferrari mechanical specifications were the most sophisticated of any car built in that period, and were the direct result of racing development. More common was the room-full-of-engineers designing, and then develop-it-on-our-proving-ground approach used by the majority of the world's automobile manufacturers.

These early Ferraris were fantastic automobiles when compared to their contemporaries. Powerful V-12 engines with performance to match, the most beautiful automotive sounds in the world, precise all-synchromesh transmissions and superb handling characteristics made the Ferrari driver king of the road.

But, they are not all that pleasant to drive by today's standards. The steering is heavy, the ride is harsh and those enormous drum brakes that look so impressive are affected by heat, cold, dirt, water and the whims of fate.

They were visually attractive cars with good lines, well-fitting body panels and leather interiors, but often looked unfinished in areas such as the engine and trunk compartments.

The 250 Europa GT set the stage, and philosophy, for Ferraris to follow; exciting, handsome, charismatic and, in reality, no better or worse than thousands of other cars. But they were fast, made beautiful noises and had no performance equal on road or track.

Two first-series Europas with the long-block Lampredi V-12, and 110-inch wheelbase. Subsequent Europa GT's had 102.3-inch wheelbase. Pininfarina photos.

Europa GT by Vignale (serial number 0359), was built for Princess Lili-
ana de Rethy. Designer Michelotti copied the wraparound windshield
so popular in the mid-fifties. Author photo.

250 Europa GT

ENGINE
Type: . . . . Colombo-designed, 60-degree V-12
Bore x stroke, mm/inches: . . . . . 73 x 58.8/2.870 x 2.315
Displacement, cc/cubic inches: 2953/180.0
Valve operation: . . . Single overhead camshaft on each bank
    with roller followers and rocker arms to inclined valves
Compression ratio: 8.5:1
Carburetion: . . . . Three Weber twin-choke, downdraft
Bhp (Mfr): . . . . 220 @ 7000

CHASSIS & DRIVETRAIN
Clutch: . . . . Twin dry-plate
Transmission: . . . Four-speed, all-synchromesh, direct drive in
    fourth
Rear suspension: . . . Live axle with semi-elliptic springs, lo-
    cated by parallel trailing arms, and lever-action shock
    absorbers
Axle ratio: . . . . 4.85, 4.57 or 4.25:1
Front suspension: . . . Independent with unequal-length A-
    arms, coil springs and lever-action shock absorbers
Frame: . . . . Welded tubular steel, ladder type

GENERAL
Wheelbase, mm/inches: 2600/102.3
Track, front, mm/inches: 1354/53.3
    rear, mm/inches: 1349/53.1
Brakes: . . . . Aluminum drums with iron liners
Tire size, front and rear: 6.00-16
Wheels: . . . . Borrani wire, center-lock, knock-off
Body builder: . . . . Pinin Farina or Vignale

Interior of de Rethy coupe was unique to this car,
yet similar to other Ferraris of the period. Full set of
instruments is Ferrari trademark. Author photo.

Colombo-designed V-12 in the Europa GT had twin distributors, driven off front of camshafts, spark plugs on the inside of the heads and single air cleaner. Author photo.

Number 0407 appears to be the transition between the Europa styling and the 250 GT. The hood slopes down to a flattened-oval air intake which would become standard. Pininfarina photo.

The Pinin Farina prototype 250 GT, number 0429GT, shared the Ferrari stand at the Geneva auto show in March 1956, with a Boano-built 250 GT cabriolet and a Pinin Farina 410 Superamerica. *Auto Italiana* reported in its April 20, 1956, issue that Ferrari would simultaneously market the Pinin Farina coupe and the Boano cabriolet.

In fact, the Boano organization built, with slight changes, the Pinin Farina-designed coupe through the 1958 models, and Farina brought out its own open car in 1957. The first appearance of a Boano-built 250 GT coupe was at the Paris Salon in October 1956.

After the 1957 models, Mario Boano left his company to work in Fiat's styling department, and Carrozzeria Boano was taken over by Luciano Pollo and Ezio Ellena. The 1958 250 GT coupes were built by a company which carried Ellena's name, but was, in fact, the same company that had built the 1956 and 1957 GT coupes. Unlike Farina, Vignale, Bertone and Ghia, Boano and Ellena never put their names on their cars; so you won't find a bodymaker's insignia on these models.

During the years of the Pinin Farina-Boano/Ellena collaboration, the Ferrari theme developed further into its present clean, simple style. The styling had evolved from the exciting, but often bizarre, designs of Michelotti (for Vignale) into the smooth sophisticated, and often understated, elegance associated with Farina.

The 1956 and 1957 Boano coupes had low roofs with side vent windows, and a few cars had a reversed shift pattern for the four-speed transmission. In 1958, in the Ellena-built coupes, the vent windows were eliminated, the roof was raised about two inches for increased headroom, and a standard shift pattern was adopted for all models.

Passenger comfort and luggage space were being improved with each successive body change, and the panel and trim fit of these Boano/Ellena-built cars was superb. A heater was standard, but no other extras were offered.

Another thing lacking in these early cars was adequate parking protection. The sides were almost flat, with no rub strip or body molding attached where it could do any good, and the bumpers were made of material only marginally thicker than body sheet metal. The bumpers were strictly decorative, not protective.

Body hardware items—door latches, window winding mechanisms, heater and controls, windshield wipers—were usually proprietary components from contemporary Fiats or Alfa Romeos. This kept original cost down a bit, and made parts replacement both easier and less expensive—then and now.

This Ferrari series was a pace-setter and style-setter, and yet, is currently one of the lowest-priced groups of the make.

Pinin Farina's 1956 prototype (0429) has break in beltline at rear door-edge, and Farina emblem on fender ahead of door. Pininfarina photo.

Boano 1957 production model has smooth beltline, no emblem. Factory photo.

Early Ferrari engines, such as this 250 GT V-12, had hairpin, or mouse-trap, valve springs. This was an idea of Gioacchino Colombo to reduce the height of the engine, by reducing the length of the valve stem. The first Ferrari engines with coil springs were the Testa Rossas, but all subsequent Ferrari engines had coil valve springs. Karl Dedolph photo.

250 GT Boano/Ellena

ENGINE

Type: . . . . Colombo-designed, 60-degree V-12
Bore x stroke, mm/inches: . . . . . . 73 x 58.8/2.870 x 2.315
Displacement, cc/cubic inches: 2953/180.0
Valve operation: . . . Single overhead camshaft on each bank with roller followers and rocker arms to inclined valves
Compression ratio: 8.5:1
Carburetion: . . . . Three Weber twin-choke, downdraft
Bhp (Mfr): . . . . 240 @ 7000

CHASSIS & DRIVETRAIN

Clutch: . . . . Twin dry-plate
Transmission: . . . Four-speed, all-synchromesh, direct drive in fourth
Rear suspension: . . . Live axle with semi-elliptic springs, located by parallel trailing arms, and lever-action shock absorbers
Axle ratio: . . . . *4.57, 4.25, 3.78 or 3.67:1
Front suspension: . . . Independent with unequal-length A-arms, coil springs and lever-action shock absorbers
Frame: . . . . Welded tubular steel, ladder type

GENERAL

Wheelbase, mm/inches: 2600/102.3
Track, front, mm/inches: 1354/53.3
    rear, mm/inches: 1349/53.1
Brakes: . . . . Aluminum drums with iron liners
Tire size, front and rear: 6.00-16
Wheels: . . . . Borrani wire, center-lock, knock-off
Body builder: . . . . . . Boano or Ellena (Pinin Farina design)
*4.00:1 added in 1957.

Trunk of the 1956-57 Boano coupe was not spacious, but there was some room for luggage behind the seats. Gas tank filler is inside trunk. Monteverdi photo.

Interior of 1958 Boano/Ellena coupe shows Veglia instruments common to Ferraris of the period, and under-dash heater as used in contemporary Alfa. Author photo.

High-roof 1958 250 GT (0821) had simple, elegant lines, and excellent panel fit throughout. Bumpers are strictly decorative. Driver visibility is superb. Author photo.

1958 Boano/Ellena high-roof design (0821) has no window vents, beltline break or emblems. Author photo.

Sports car racing had progressed so far by 1955 that the cars were virtually two-passenger Grand Prix cars. After the tragic Le Mans accident in 1955, where one driver and seventy-nine spectators died, there was a clamor to return to the classic type of racing. As a result, the Fédération Internationale de l'Automobile (FIA) established new Grand Touring classes for 1956. Ferrari, with help from Pinin Farina, was ready.

Farina had built lightweight aluminum bodies on Ferrari chassis since 1952, but displayed his best design to date at the Geneva show in March 1956.

These 250 GT long-wheelbase (102.3 inches) berlinettas, slightly changed from the show car, were built by Scaglietti to Farina's design, and became the customer competition car for 1956-59. The cars in this series all had odd serial numbers, making them 'production' road cars, and received FIA homologation because the mechanical specifications were identical to the Boano/Ellena coupes being built at the same time. Only the bodies were different.

Weight was saved by the use of aluminum for the body, instead of steel as on the road cars; perspex windows, instead of tempered safety glass; virtually no interior hardware or trim; and the hood lifted off to save the weight of hinges.

The GT berlinettas started out with exposed headlights slightly recessed into the front fenders. Subsequent models had the headlights moved further into the fenders, and were covered by molded perspex which was faired into the fender shape. In 1959, a small chrome bezel surrounded a more conventional headlamp mounting.

Mechanical components of this series were almost all interchangeable with other contemporary 250 GT's, but the handmade body parts wouldn't interchange. The panels were smooth, and fit well to each other, but a door from one car wouldn't even come close to fitting the door opening in the body of another look-alike GT berlinetta.

Because the engine and chassis were the same as the production coupes, the berlinettas could be driven in town as easily as any contemporary car, and yet were tough competitors in racing. Oliver Gendebien finished third overall in the 1957 Mille Miglia, driving a 250 GT berlinetta, beating a large number of sports racing cars.

Because of its road/racing concept, there were no creature comforts offered. The lack of interior insulation would probably make a radio a worthless addition because passengers wouldn't be able to enjoy it. The enjoyment of this car comes from the pleasure of driving it.

Early in 1959, a variation of the 250 GT ''Tour de France'' appeared. The chassis was unchanged, but the bodywork (also Farina-designed, Scaglietti-built) was softer and more rounded than previous versions. In addition to the changes in contours, this interim model had roll-up windows with vent wings, and quarter windows, where before there had been various louvered arrangements.

Pinin Farina displayed the first berlinetta in the fall of 1955. It had louvers behind the door, tailfins and a busy grille design. Pininfarina photo.

At Geneva, in the spring of 1956, another Pinin Farina berlinetta appeared, still with louvers, high rear fenders but no fins, and different, busy grille. Pininfarina photo.

250 GT berlinetta (LWB)
Tour de France

ENGINE
Type: . . . . Colombo-designed, 60-degree V-12
Bore x stroke, mm/inches: . . . . . 73 x 58.8/2.870 x 2.315
Displacement, cc/cubic inches: 2953/180.0
Valve operation: . . . Single overhead camshaft on each bank
    with roller followers and rocker arms to inclined valves
Compression ratio: 8.57:1
Carburetion: . . . . Three Weber twin-choke, downdraft
Bhp (Mfr): . . . . 260 @ 7000

CHASSIS & DRIVETRAIN
Clutch: . . . . *Single dry-plate
Transmission: . . . Four-speed, all-synchromesh, direct drive in
    fourth
Rear suspension: . . . Live axle with semi-elliptic springs, lo-
cated by parallel trailing arms, and lever-action shock
absorbers
Axle ratio: . . . . 4.57, 4.25, 4.00, 3.78 or 3.67:1
Front suspension: . . . Independent with unequal-length A-
    arms, coil springs and lever-action shock absorbers
Frame: . . . . Welded tubular steel, ladder type

GENERAL
Wheelbase, mm/inches: 2600/102.3
Track, front, mm/inches: 1354/53.3
    rear, mm/inches: 1349/53.1
Brakes: . . . . Aluminum drums with iron liners
Tire size, front and rear: 6.00-16
Wheels: . . . . Borrani wire, center-lock, knock-off
Body builder: . . . . Scaglietti (Pinin Farina design)
*1956-57 berlinettas had twin-disc clutches; 1958-59 models had a
single-disc clutch.

By 1957, the Scaglietti-built (to Pinin Farina design) 250 GT berlinetta was starting to look right. Extra lights were for rallies and 24-hour races. Ferrari photo.

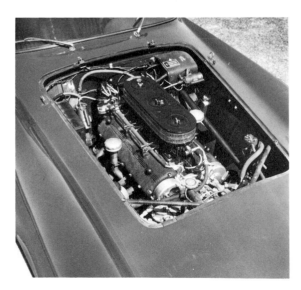

Same basic car and engine, in two configurations. The 1958 model (0925) has the single air cleaner and was primarily a road car; while the late 1958-59 model, right, has the cold-air box seen on competition cars. Author photos.

Car with serial number 0925 is a 1958-model 250 GT berlinetta. This one was Bill Harrah's first Ferrari and is still in Harrah's Automobile Collection in Reno. It was a road car and used by him as daily transportation when new. It is fairly luxurious for this model. Author photo.

Number 1353 is a 1959 250 GT berlinetta and is fairly typical of the series. It was a competition car and has a stark interior. Author photos.

The 250 GT berlinetta interior is all business. Gauges include 300 kph speedometer, 8000 rpm tach, water temperature, oil pressure, ammeter, fuel and clock. Author photo.

A rare model, the 250 GT berlinetta with body by Zagato. These were
lightweight cars for competition, and were successfully campaigned by
private entrants in Europe. Strother MacMinn photo.

The 'interim' long-wheelbase berlinetta displayed the softer body lines
of the upcoming 250 GT short-wheelbase model, while sharing the
chassis with the older cars. Author photo.

Even though open Ferraris had been seen since the first Ferrari in 1947, it wasn't until ten years later that convertible Ferraris were produced in series.

Farina chose the 1957 Geneva auto show in March to show a 250 GT cabriolet. This car (0655GT) later became the personal transportation for Ferrari team driver Peter Collins. On the right side, it looked much as subsequent cabriolets would look; but on the left side, the door was cut down much in the manner of the T series MG's.

Designers of these early cabriolets seemed to be groping for a look, and they found it by the time the fourth one had been built—the design became classic.

This short series of cars is characterized by vertical front bumperettes and horizontal rear bumpers, no side vents on the fenders (although a few of the very early examples had vents similar to the 410 Superamerica) and, until the last of the series, each had headlights covered by clear perspex faired into the front fender lines. Toward the end of this series, in 1958, the headlights moved out onto the front of the fenders, with no covering, and the front bumper became a horizontal crossbar which was to become the norm.

The cabriolet chassis was identical to that of the Boano coupes being produced at the same time: welded oval tubular steel ladder-type frame with independent front and live rear axle, and drum brakes. The Colombo engine had the spark plugs located inside the vee, and had a single distributor at the back of the engine.

Peter Collins's car was equipped with Dunlop disc brakes at the Dunlop headquarters in England. Ferrari later 'borrowed' the brakes from Collins's car to install on a racing car. This was the first use of disc brakes on a Ferrari; they were later to become standard equipment.

Keeping track of Ferraris is a confusing task. For example, the Spyder California was in production before production stopped on the cabriolet. Both are convertibles in the American idiom, with roll-up windows, and the basic body design of the two is similar enough to look identical to the uninitiated. Remember, though, that the cabriolets were designed and built by Pinin Farina, while the Spyder California is a Pinin Farina design built by Scaglietti. Look for the body-maker's insignia.

The cabriolet also has an all-steel body, whereas the California can be steel with aluminum doors, hood and deck lid, or all aluminum. There will be little difference in handling or driveability, except in racing conditions where the lighter weight of the California will be an advantage.

The Spyder California will be more valuable because of its dual-purpose concept. It was actually advertised by Ferrari as a road car you can race, which the cabriolets were not.

The first Pinin Farina spyder (not to be confused with the Spyder California) was number 0655, built in 1957. Very little of the styling was carried over to future models. Pininfarina photo.

Number 0795, built later in 1957, had more of the upcoming characteristics, but still had no window vents. Karl Dedolph photo.

A 1958 Pinin Farina spyder in front of the Ferrari factory in Maranello.
A Pinin Farina 250 GT coupe is in the background. Factory photo by A.
Villani & Figli.

250 GT cabriolet—Series I

ENGINE

Type: . . . . Colombo-designed, 60-degree V-12
Bore x stroke, mm/inches: . . . . . . 73 x 58.8/2.870 x 2.315
Displacement, cc/cubic inches: 2953/180.0
Valve operation: . . . Single overhead camshaft on each bank
    with roller followers and rocker arms to inclined valves
Compression ratio: 8.5:1
Carburetion: . . . . Three Weber twin-choke, downdraft
Bhp (Mfr): . . . . 240 @ 7000

CHASSIS & DRIVETRAIN

Clutch: . . . . Twin dry-plate
Transmission: . . . Four-speed, all-synchromesh, direct drive in
    fourth
Rear suspension: . . . Live axle with semi-elliptic springs, lo-
    cated by parallel trailing arms, and lever-action shock
    absorbers
Axle ratio: . . . . 4.57, 4.25, 3.78 or 3.67:1
Front suspension: . . . Independent with unequal-length A-
    arms, coil springs and lever-action shock absorbers
Frame: . . . . Welded tubular steel, ladder type

GENERAL

Wheelbase, mm/inches: 2600/102.3
Track, front, mm/inches: 1354/53.3
    rear, mm/inches: 1349/53.1
Brakes: . . . . Aluminum drums with iron liners
Tire size, front and rear: 6.00-16
Wheels: . . . . Borrani wire, center-lock, knock-off
Body builder: . . . . Pinin Farina

A Speciale show car for Turin in 1957 was this Pinin Farina spyder number 0709. Montovani/Pininfarina photos.

Although the first Spyder California was built in December 1957, *this* model went into production in May 1958. The chassis and engine were identical to that used in the 250 GT long-wheelbase berlinettas and, like the berlinetta, the design was by Pinin Farina and the actual construction was by Scaglietti.

The California came about because of a request from John von Neumann, who was the West Coast Ferrari distributor at that time. Pinin Farina-built cabriolets had been offered since mid-1957, but were strictly touring cars, complete with full interior trim and with no consideration given to light weight or competition. Von Neumann felt that an open car with the characteristics of the lighter berlinettas would be very popular here, and the factory obliged by creating the Spyder California.

It is difficult for the uninitiated to tell the California and cabriolet apart; but, basically, the cabrio has a wider grille, vertical front bumperettes (until mid-1958), faired-in headlights, wraparound windshield with side windwings, no air outlets in the front fender sides and a rounded rear fender design with the lights at the top.

The California has a narrower, oval grille opening, side vents in the front fenders, a less-pronounced wraparound windshield and vertical taillights at the top of the rear fenders. Other than the top, the body is very similar to the 250 GT berlinetta.

Like other 250 GT's of the period, including the berlinetta, drum brakes were still used, as were lever-action shock absorbers. In fact, all mechanical specifications were the same for the California, berlinetta, cabriolet and coupe that were built at the same time, even with three different body builders (Pinin Farina, Boano/Ellena, and Scaglietti).

The combination of rarity (less than fifty long-wheelbase Californias were built), competition capability and appearance cause these to be some of the most sought-after Ferraris. They looked great when they were built, and they still look great today. Not everyone wants open-air driving, but for those who do, this is a wonderful car.

A 1958 long-wheelbase Spyder California (0923) has the lines that
were to be characteristic of this series. Marshall Mathews photos.

A 1959 LWB Spyder (1501) has front bumper over-riders and driving lights in grille, but otherwise is like the 1958 LWB. Pete Coltrin photos.

Engine compartment of 1501. The owner has removed the air cleaner, probably for competition. Twin Marelli distributors were standard on this model. Pete Coltrin photo.

Minor differences can be seen in the interiors of 0923, above, and 1501, such as door trim and placement of window crank. Marshall Mathews photo.

Clean, classic lines of the LWB Spyder California, built by Scaglietti to Pinin Farina design. Karl Dedolph photo.

250 GT Spyder California (LWB)

ENGINE

Type: . . . . Colombo-designed, 60-degree V-12
Bore x stroke, mm/inches: . . . . . 73 x 58.8/2.870 x 2.315
Displacement, cc/cubic inches: 2953/180.0
Valve operation: . . . Single overhead camshaft on each bank
   with roller followers and rocker arms to inclined valves
Compression ratio: 8.57:1
Carburetion: . . . . Three Weber twin-choke, downdraft
Bhp (Mfr): . . . . 260 @ 7000

CHASSIS & DRIVETRAIN

Clutch: . . . . Twin dry-plate
Transmission: . . . Four-speed, all-synchromesh, direct drive in
   fourth

Rear suspension: . . . Live axle with semi-elliptic springs, located by parallel trailing arms, and lever-action shock
   absorbers
Axle ratio: . . . . 4.57, 4.25, 4.00, 3.78 or 3.67:1
Front suspension: . . . Independent with unequal-length A-
   arms, coil springs and lever-action shock absorbers
Frame: . . . . Welded tubular steel, ladder type

GENERAL

Wheelbase, mm/inches: 2600/102.3
Track, front, mm/inches: 1354/53.3
   rear, mm/inches: 1349/53.1
Brakes: . . . . Aluminum drums with iron liners
Tire size, front and rear: 6.00-16
Wheels: . . . . Borrani wire, center-lock, knock-off
Body builder: . . . . Scaglietti (Pinin Farina design)

A new Pinin Farina-bodied 250 GT coupe was shown at the Paris Salon in October 1958. It was a 1959 model, and would replace the Boano/Ellena coupe as the standard production Ferrari road car through 1961.

The first cars in this series shared most mechanical components with the 1958 cars—drum brakes, lever-action Houdaille shock absorbers, four-speed transmission and spark plugs located inside the vee of the engine. One initial difference was that twin Marelli distributors replaced the single distributor used previously. This was welcome because the single unit had a habit of arcing across the contacts inside the distributor cap because the contacts were too close together. This model also had the first fresh-air heater used on a Ferrari.

The Pinin Farina body remained unchanged during the model run; but in 1960, mechanical changes were made which vastly improved the car. Spark plugs were moved to the outside of the heads and siamesed intake ports were abandoned in favor of individual ports; disc brakes replaced the sometimes dodgy drum brakes; tubular shocks were made standard equipment; overdrive was added to the four-speed transmission; and a single-disc clutch replaced the twin-disc unit previously used.

A large-section tubular frame connected the independent front suspension, with its unequal-length A-arms and coil springs, to the live rear axle which had semi-elliptic springs and was located by Ferrari's twin parallel trailing arms.

Styling of the new 250 GT was not as exciting as some other Farina designs, before or since; but it was clean and elegant, and has worn well for the last twenty years. The coupe body is almost identical to the cabriolet—the main difference being the raised rear fenders of the open cars.

Passenger space and comfort were the best of any Ferrari (other than the Superamericas) up to this point, as was luggage accommodation. These features, along with better brakes, make PF coupes some of the best touring cars of the era.

My experience of maintaining a 250 GT (actually a 1958 Ellena coupe, which had the same mechanical specifications as the first PF coupes) taught me to change a set of spark plugs in forty-five minutes, after a year's practice. My first Ferrari plug change took an hour and a half—partly from inexperience and partly from fear of cross-threading the plugs in their seemingly inaccessible location.

And the brakes—awful. I developed the practice of gently riding the brakes for about the first mile or so in the morning because those fourteen-inch drums, when cold, wouldn't begin to stop the car in a straight line. They did a pretty fair job once they were warmed up, however.

For these reasons alone, I recommend looking for a late 250 PF if this model is in your range of interest and income.

The first pre-production prototype set the style for the series, which continued for three years with about 350 being built. Pininfarina photo.

The second pre-production prototype was shown in June 1958. By now, the design was set. Pininfarina photos.

This special-bodied 250 GT (0853) was built in 1958 for Prince Bertil of Sweden. Pininfarina photo.

250 GT PF coupe

ENGINE

Type: . . . . Colombo-designed, 60-degree V-12
Bore x stroke, mm/inches: . . . . . 73 x 58.8/2.870 x 2.315
Displacement, cc/cubic inches: 2953/180.0
Valve operation: . . . Single overhead camshaft on each bank
    with roller followers and rocker arms to inclined valves
Compression ratio: 8.57:1
Carburetion: . . . . Three Weber twin-choke, downdraft
Bhp (Mfr): . . . . 240 @ 7000

CHASSIS & DRIVETRAIN

Clutch: . . . . *Single dry-plate
Transmission: . . . *Four-speed, all-synchromesh, direct drive
    in fourth
Rear suspension: . . . *Live axle with semi-elliptic springs, lo-
    cated by parallel trailing arms, and telescopic shock ab-
    sorbers
Axle ratio: . . . . 4.57, 4.25, 4.00, 3.78 or 3.67:1
Front suspension: . . . *independent with unequal-length A-
    arms, coil springs and telescopic shock absorbers
Frame: . . . . Welded tubular steel, ladder type

GENERAL

Wheelbase, mm/inches: 2600/102.3
Track, front, mm/inches: 1354/53.3
    rear, mm/inches: 1349/53.1
Brakes: . . . . *Disc
Tire size, front and rear: *6.00-16
Wheels: . . . . Borrani wire, center-lock, knock-off
Body builder: . . . . *Pinin Farina
*1960-61 cars had overdrive, 1958-59 models had lever-action shock
absorbers, drum brakes and a twin-disc clutch. Tire sizes were at
times 185-400, 185-15 or 6.00-16. Pinin Farina became Pininfarina
in 1961.

Standard engine compartment of the Ferrari V-12; three Weber downdrafts covered by a single air cleaner. This was the first Ferrari with fresh-air ventilation and heater, with the air intake at the base of the windshield. *Road & Track* photo.

A special car was built in 1958 for an old customer. The body is standard 250 GT, but the bumpers were vertical rather than horizontal, the lower body panels were chrome and the interior had true bucket seats. Pininfarina photo.

Early 1960 Pinin Farina coupe. The interior was becoming even more luxurious in the Grand Touring tradition. Seatbacks were adjustable for rake. *Road & Track* photo.

In October 1959, at the Paris Salon, a shortened version (commonly referred to as the SWB—short wheelbase) of the interim car was displayed. Front and rear shapes were almost identical to the interim berlinettas, but the 94.5-inch wheelbase necessitated elimination of the quarter windows, with a subsequent improvement in looks.

Most SWB bodies were steel with aluminum doors, hood and trunk lid; but some all-aluminum bodies were built for the serious competitor during the three-year model run.

The Colombo-designed engine was still used and all examples had twelve intake ports with the plugs on the outside of the heads, coil valve springs replaced the 'hairpin' or 'mousetrap' springs previously used, and there were four studs around each cylinder instead of three—greatly improving compression sealing. Disc brakes and tubular shock absorbers also became standard.

As a result of the increased horsepower, shorter and lighter chassis and better brakes, the SWB 250 GT was faster and handled better than its predecessors, making it formidable competition in any type of event.

These competition-oriented GT berlinettas, which carried odd serial numbers representative of the road cars, were raced and rallied with great success. The Tour de France, which was a week-long rally around France, with eight timed events (six races and two hillclimbs) interspersed into the rally, was won by Ferrari so many times that the long-wheelbase 250 GT was called the Tour de France model. The SWB continued the winning ways.

Ferraris won the Tour de France in 1951, were second in 1952 and 1953, and won in 1956, '57, '58, '59, '60 (1st, 2nd & 3rd) and '61 (1-2-3-4). Because of their favored status with competitors, the cars were made in both left- and right-hand-drive versions.

All 250 GT berlinettas, with long or short wheelbase, are desirable collector cars because of their handsome lines and excellent performance. They are docile enough to drive in traffic, but fast enough to be in the winner's circle after a race. Because of their desirability, they have appreciated tremendously in the last few years and it appears there is no end in sight.

These berlinettas are some of the few cars that are worth salvaging from a 'basket case' because the end result is worth the cost and effort.

Certain examples of the 250 GT SWB were built with large fuel tanks, necessitating the spare tire resting directly under the rear window. Standard engines were rated at 280 bhp, 20 bhp higher than the standard 250 GT of the time. Others had tuned 300 bhp Testa Rossa engines with six carburetors. This SWB, built in 1960, bears the serial number 1993GT. Stan Nowak photo.

The man himself. Enzo Ferrari at the wheel of a 250 GT berlinetta. Pete Coltrin photo.

Interior of the 250 SWB (3337) left no provision for adding creature amenities, so this owner mounted a radio on top of the transmission tunnel. Author photo.

250 GT berlinetta (SWB)

ENGINE

Type: . . . . Colombo-designed, 60-degree V-12
Bore x stroke, mm/inches: . . . . . . 73 x 58.8/2.870 x 2.315
Displacement, cc/cubic inches: 2953/180.0
Valve operation: . . . Single overhead camshaft on each bank
 with roller followers and rocker arms to inclined valves
Compression ratio: 9.2:1
Carburetion: . . . . Three Weber twin-choke, downdraft
Bhp (Mfr): . . . . 280 @ 7000

CHASSIS & DRIVETRAIN

Clutch: . . . . Single dry-plate
Transmission: . . . Four-speed, all-synchromesh, direct drive in
 fourth
Rear suspension: . . . Live axle with semi-elliptic springs, lo-
 cated by parallel trailing arms, and telescopic shock ab-
 sorbers
Axle ratio: . . . . . 4.57, 4.25, 4.00, 3.78, 3.67, 3.55 or 3.44:1
Front suspension: . . . Independent with unequal-length A-
 arms, coil springs and telescopic shock absorbers
Frame: . . . . Welded tubular steel, ladder type

GENERAL

Wheelbase, mm/inches: 2400/94.5
Track, front, mm/inches: 1354/53.3
 rear, mm/inches: 1349/53.1
Brakes: . . . . Disc
Tire size, front and rear: *6.00-16
Wheels: . . . . Borrani wire, center-lock, knock-off
Body builder: . . . . Scaglietti (Pinin Farina design)
*Pre-1960 cars. 1960 and later had 175-400 or 185-15 tires.

Front and rear (3337) show clean shapes with general lack of ornamentation. Body is by Scaglietti to a Pininfarina design. Author photos.

The bodies on the 1960 and '61 SWB berlinettas were the same, in shape and general detailing; but the 1961 had opening vent wings, and the 1960 (1993) did not. Pininfarina photo.

One of the best all-around cars of the period, the 250 GT short-wheel-base berlinetta, was at home on either road or track. Bodies were made of steel with aluminum doors, hood and trunk lid; although the serious competitor could have an all-aluminum body. Karl Dedolph photo.

Serial Nos. 1537GT-3803GT

Realizing the confusion that could exist between the cabriolet and Spyder, Pinin Farina took steps to separate the look of the two cars. This was fairly simple, as the California had been derived from the long-wheelbase berlinetta (both mechanically and visually); and the cabriolet was closely identified with the coupes, so the styling of the cabriolet became more like the 1959 Pinin Farina coupe.

Most Ferrari enthusiasts think the Spyders are better looking than the cabriolets, and the Spyder *does* have slightly better performance, so it is the more popular of the two designs. The Pinin Farina version, however, was conceived as a semi-luxury touring car and had better interior appointments, more soundproofing and was better suited to the average Ferrari customer for everyday use.

The cabriolet is an elegant and understated design which, if you like it at all, wears well and withstands the test of time.

Like other Ferraris, running changes were made at various times, including the switch to disc brakes; telescopic shock absorbers replaced the Houdaille lever-action units; overdrive was added to the four-speed transmission; and twin distributors replaced the single unit used initially.

The cabriolets, both Series I and II, are relatively good buys if one has to have a Ferrari. They look good, will do almost anything the other models will do (and do it as well), and the investment is lower, because other models are more popular and have appreciated faster.

Getting back to whether you want a car to drive, or a show piece—the cabriolets are (in my opinion) 'drivers.' You wouldn't have to constantly hover over it and have a heart attack if someone touches it, or parks too close.

Given a choice between an early and a late version of the same model (and barring some extraordinary bargain price on one or the other), always opt for the later car. It will have running mechanical changes that invariably make it a better car. The 250 cabriolet is a case in point; adoption of disc brakes, tubular shock absorbers, twin distributors and overdrive all make the car more pleasant to drive than earlier models. Visually, you'd be hard put to tell them apart without opening the hood or looking underneath the car.

Also, when Ferrari moved the spark plugs from inside the vee to the outside of the heads, it allowed the redesign of the cylinder head which reduced the possibility of blown head gaskets. These later engines are not only more reliable, but are easier to service if something does go wrong.

Pinin Farina cabriolet 250 GT shown with optional, removable hardtop. Classic lines were and are typical of Farina's restrained design approach. Pininfarina photos.

A Pinin Farina 250 GT cabriolet inside the massive Farina factory in Torino, Italy. Pininfarina photo.

A rare Series II Pinin Farina cabriolet with the flat hood (without air-scoop) as used on the 250 GT coupes. Pininfarina photo.

A 250 GT *cabriolet speciale,* number 1737GT, was built on a short-wheelbase chassis and had coachwork similar to that appearing on several 400 Superamericas (see Chapter 21). Pininfarina photos.

250 GT cabriolet—Series II

ENGINE

Type: . . . . Colombo-designed, 60-degree V-12
Bore x stroke, mm/inches: . . . . . 73 x 58.8/2.870 x 2.315
Displacement, cc/cubic inches: 2953/180.0
Valve operation: . . . Single overhead camshaft on each bank
　　with roller followers and rocker arms to inclined valves
Compression ratio: 8.57:1
Carburetion: . . . . Three Weber twin-choke, downdraft
Bhp (Mfr): . . . . 260 @ 7000

CHASSIS & DRIVETRAIN

Clutch: . . . . Single dry-plate
Transmission: . . . Four-speed, all-synchromesh, direct drive in
　　fourth with electrically operated overdrive (28.2%) fifth
Rear suspension: . . . Live axle with semi-elliptic springs, lo-
cated by parallel trailing arms, and telescopic shock absorbers
Axle ratio: . . . . 4.57, 4.25, 4.00, 3.78 or 3.67:1
Front suspension: . . . Independent with unequal-length A-arms, coil springs and telescopic shock absorbers
Frame: . . . . Welded tubular steel, ladder type

GENERAL

Wheelbase, mm/inches: 2600/102.3
Track, front, mm/inches: 1354/53.3
　　rear, mm/inches: 1349/53.1
Brakes: . . . . Disc
Tire size, front and rear: *6.00-16
Wheels: . . . . Borrani wire, center-lock, knock-off
Body builder: . . . . Pinin Farina
*Later models had 185-15 tires.

CHAPTER 9
250 GT SPYDER CALIFORNIA
1960-63

Serial Nos. 1795GT-4137GT

Production of the short-wheelbase Spyder Californias spanned the period from May 1960 to February 1963. During that two-and-a-half-year period only about fifty of the model were built.

Like its predecessor, the long-wheelbase California, chassis specifications were almost identical to the berlinetta that paralleled it in production: the short-wheelbase (94.5 inches) berlinetta which had gone into production in 1959.

Unlike the long-wheelbase cars, however, the body shape of the SWB California was more like the long-wheelbase California—shortened to fit the eight-inch-shorter wheelbase—and bore no resemblance to the SWB berlinetta whose chassis it shared. The SWB California body design was a continuation of the LWB Pinin Farina shape, and built by Scaglietti, in Modena.

The short-wheelbase California had more in common with its predecessor than looks and general mechanical specifications, however, as it had even better competition capabilities because of its lighter weight and better handling qualities.

The engine was the outside plug 250 V-12, and tubular shocks and disc brakes were standard. The SWB would go, turn and stop; and it looked great! It was, in fact, advertised as a car that could be driven in normal daily use, or raced. Not too many owners chose to race the Spyder Californias, as they were purchased by customers who wanted the 'rub-off' from the implied association with a model built as a semi-competition car. The fact that they *didn't* race it was less important than the fact that they *could* race it if they wanted to. Most owners rightly thought that the California was just too pretty to put on a track where it would get damaged from gravel thrown by a competitor's tires or, worse, get bumped.

As good as they were, and are, the ride and handling is vintage fifties, and by today's more demanding standards, they don't measure up. The Californias are easy-to-drive cars and quite comfortable in most driving conditions, but don't expect one to handle like a later V-12 with independent suspension, or like a 308 mid-engined V-8.

Vintage or not, the short-wheelbase Californias are some of the most sought-after Ferraris. Because of their performance and appearance, combined with scarcity, prices are skyrocketing.

The classic beauty of the SWB can be seen in these photos of George Carrick's car taken by Clive Clark.

A 1961 short-wheelbase Spyder California (3077) is one of the prettiest of Ferraris, and it looks as good when it's 20 years old as it did when new. Vittorio L. Roveda photos.

Things to watch for: This SWB Spyder has wrong steering wheel; rear-view mirror has been moved from top of dash to windshield; outside fender mirrors are aftermarket accessory mirrors; Ferrari name should *not* appear above emblem in front of hood; and wheels are wrong. None of this makes any difference in driveability, but disqualifies it as an original car. Author photos.

Some short-wheelbase Spyder Californias didn't have covered headlights or side vents in front fenders. Author photo.

250 GT Spyder California (SWB)

ENGINE
Type: . . . . Colombo-designed, 60-degree V-12
Bore x stroke, mm/inches: . . . . . . 73 x 58.8/2.870 x 2.315
Displacement, cc/cubic inches: 2953/180.0
Valve operation: . . . Single overhead camshaft on each bank with roller followers and rocker arms to inclined valves
Compression ratio: 9.2:1
Carburetion: . . . . Three Weber twin-choke, downdraft
Bhp (Mfr): . . . . 280 @ 7000

CHASSIS & DRIVETRAIN
Clutch: . . . . Single dry-plate
Transmission: . . . Four-speed, all-synchromesh, direct drive in fourth
Rear suspension: . . . Live axle with semi-elliptic springs, located by parallel trailing arms, and telescopic shock absorbers
Axle ratio: . . . . . 4.57, 4.25, 4.00, 3.78, 3.67, 3.55 or 3.44:1
Front suspension: . . . Independent with unequal-length A-arms, coil springs and telescopic shock absorbers
Frame: . . . . Welded tubular steel, ladder type

GENERAL
Wheelbase, mm/inches: 2400/94.5
Track, front, mm/inches: 1354/53.3
      rear, mm/inches: 1349/53.1
Brakes: . . . . Disc
Tire size, front and rear: *6.00-16
Wheels: . . . . Borrani wire, center-lock, knock-off
Body builder: . . . . Scaglietti (Pinin Farina design)
*Pre-1960 cars. 1960 and later had 175-400 or 185-15 tires.

Serial Nos. 4103GT-5955GT

Paris, October 1962. At the annual auto show, Ferrari and Pininfarina once again introduced a new car, the 250 GT/L, which became known unofficially as the Lusso, for luxury.

Combining design elements from the competition-oriented short-wheelbase berlinettas and the 250 GTO, it was, and is, one of the handsomest Ferraris. No, make that one of the most handsome *cars* ever built. During its two-year life span, approximately 350 Lussos were built.

The Lusso chassis was, again, a fairly standard Ferrari design, with unequal-length A-arms and coil spring front suspension. The rear suspension was the tried-and-true semi-elliptic springs with axle location by parallel trailing arms on each side. However, two new features for a Ferrari road car were seen at the back: the telescopic shock absorbers had concentric 'helper' springs wound around them, and the axle's lateral location was by Watt linkage. Both features were borrowed from the GTO. Disc brakes were also standard.

Lusso bodies were built by Scaglietti to Pininfarina's design and were of steel, with aluminum doors, hood and trunk lid. I have heard that there were a few all-aluminum Lusso bodies, but I've never seen one. Like too many other Ferraris, the beautiful bodywork is almost unprotected from potential parking damage. The bumpers are, at best, decorative. This wouldn't stop me from buying one, but would make me very cautious about where I parked it.

The seats are genuine bucket type (unlike most previous Ferrari road cars), comparable to those found in the GT berlinettas. The seats are adjustable fore and aft, but have no back rake adjustment and don't tilt forward—so loading luggage into the area behind the seats requires physical strength and dexterity.

The instrument panel is unique to the Lusso, with a large speedometer and tachometer in the center of the panel—angled toward the driver—and the five smaller gauges mounted right in front of the driver. Vision is superb, with lots of glass area and minimal interference from windshield posts or quarter panels.

I've not spent much time in a Lusso, but several owners have complained to me about excessive noise in the cockpit due to the paucity of insulation and the low rear axle gearing (high ratio) which causes the engine to run at higher rpm than should be needed for easy cruising. If this isn't bothersome to you, then don't worry about it. If it is bothersome, the first time the rear axle needs major work, investigate different gear ratios for the ring and pinion. On the other hand, some owners also complain of an excessively high first gear, making the Lusso a little difficult to start smoothly from a stop.

Road & Track editors conducted a road test of a five-year-old Lusso in the June 1969 issue and reported that ''the wood-rimmed steering wheel is rather high, nearly vertical and isn't adjustable in any way'' and although the seatbacks weren't adjustable ''the brake and clutch pedals have a simple adjustment that allows moving the pads fore and aft about two inches.''

During the performance tests, which netted a standing-start quarter-mile time of 16.1 seconds (91 miles per hour at the end of the quarter), they discovered the marginal clutch had started to slip after several consecutive fast starts. And, ''The speedometer is as optimistic as in most Ferraris.'' It has been my experience that Ferrari (and Maserati and Lamborghini) speedometers run anywhere from five to fifteen percent optimistic.

None of these factors would deter me from investing in a Lusso. It is still one of the most desirable of Ferraris.

The 1962-64 250 GT berlinetta Lusso was, and is, one of the handsomest Ferraris. Its classic lines, plus its rarity make it one of the most desirable of Ferraris. Pininfarina photo.

The Lusso interior is unique among Ferraris, with the speedometer and tach in the center of the panel and the smaller instruments in front of the driver. Ed Niles photo.

250 GT berlinetta Lusso

ENGINE

Type: . . . . Colombo-designed, 60-degree V-12
Bore x stroke, mm/inches: . . . . . . 73 x 58.8/2.870 x 2.315
Displacement, cc/cubic inches: 2953/180.0
Valve operation: . . . Single overhead camshaft on each bank
    with roller followers and rocker arms to inclined valves
Compression ratio: 9.3:1
Carburetion: . . . . Three Weber twin-choke, downdraft
Bhp (Mfr): . . . . 250 @ 7000

CHASSIS & DRIVETRAIN

Clutch: . . . . Single dry-plate
Transmission: . . . Four-speed, all-synchromesh, direct drive in
    fourth
Rear suspension: . . . Live axle with semi-elliptic springs, lo-
    cated by parallel trailing arms, and telescopic shock ab-
    sorbers
Axle ratio: . . . . 4.00 or 3.78:1
Front suspension: . . . Independent with unequal-length A-
    arms, coil springs and telescopic shock absorbers
Frame: . . . . Welded tubular steel, ladder type

GENERAL

Wheelbase, mm/inches: 2400/94.5
Track, front, mm/inches: 1395/55.0
    rear, mm/inches: 1387/54.6
Brakes: . . . . Disc
Tire size, front and rear: 185SP-15
Wheels: . . . . Borrani wire, center-lock, knock-off
Body builder: . . . . Scaglietti (Pininfarina design)

Lusso passengers learned to travel light. With spare tire and tool kit in trunk, there was little room for anything else. Some luggage can be accommodated behind seats. *Road & Track* photo.

Lusso engine compartment. Two distributors at the back, two breathers and two oil filters at the front. Vintage Car Store photo.

A special Lusso (4335) was built in 1963 for the personal use of Giovanni Battista Giuseppe "Pinin" Farina (who changed his surname through Italian legal process in 1961 to Pininfarina). This car has a pronounced hood bulge, no vent wing on the driver's door, 400 SA-type door handles, a slightly larger spoiler on the rear and the large instruments in front of the driver instead of the center of the panel as on the production Lussos. Pininfarina photos.

Serial Nos. 5003GT-9079GT

Two new Ferraris made their debut at the 1964 Paris Salon: the 275 GTB and GTS. The chassis were identical, with the now-typical welded steel tubular frame, full independent suspension with unequal-length A-arms front and rear, disc brakes and tubular shock absorbers. The engines were also identical 3.3-liter V-12's of Colombo origin, but the berlinetta engine produced 280 horsepower while the spyder engine was rated at 260.

Both models had a five-speed transmission mounted in unit with the rear axle. The clutch and bell housing were at the engine. With the rear-mounted gearbox came independent rear suspension, making the 275 GTB the first street Ferrari to be so equipped.

The bodywork was completely different on the two cars; the spyder evolved from the 330 GT 2+2 (Pininfarina designed and built), but the berlinetta body was a completely new shape—a replacement for the Lusso with softer, more rounded curves, designed by Pininfarina but built by Scaglietti.

The 275 GTB was intended for either touring or racing, and the customer had the option of either three Weber carburetors (with which the GTB was homologated for competition by the FIA) or six. The body could be steel and aluminum or all-aluminum. Campagnolo alloy wheels were standard, but Borrani wire wheels were an option.

The body shape remained almost unchanged throughout the model run, but minor changes were in evidence when the Series II cars were shown at Frankfurt in 1965. The headlight covers no longer had chrome rims, the vent wing was missing from the driver's window and a bulge appeared on the hood to cover the carburetors. At the rear, the trunk lid hinges were on the outside of the body to allow more interior space. At the Paris show a month later, the front of the body had been lengthened and had a smaller air intake.

By the time the Series II 275 GTB was shown at the Brussels show in January 1966, the car had new alloy wheels, and the driveshaft was encased in a torque tube. Approximately 250 Series I and about two hundred Series II 275 GTB's were built.

In the spring of 1966, a special version, the 275 GTB/C, was built in very limited numbers (about a dozen) with serial numbers between 9007 and 9085. These 275's had special camshafts, valves, pistons, crankshaft and carburetors, and a dry-sump lubrication system. The bodies were aluminum and the cars were created expressly for competition.

The 275 series marked the progressive change in Ferrari design philosophy from thinly disguised racers to comfortable and luxurious transportation vehicles. Because of the chassis changes—primarily the four-wheel independent suspension—the 275's were not only faster, but more comfortable than their predecessors. The 275 series offered an extremely high-speed touring car (remember they were designed when there were no speed limits in most of Europe and the U.S. hadn't gone to 55 mph yet) which gave the driver and passenger the utmost feeling of confidence. You could drive all day as fast as you cared to and arrive at your destination without the fatigue normally associated with this sort of endeavor.

The one drawback of the 275 was the somewhat notchy shift mechanism of the rear-mounted transmission. Earlier Ferraris with the transmission mounted at the back of the engine were much easier to shift. The trade-off, however, is on the side of the 275.

A competition version, the 275 GTB/C, was built in limited numbers. All basic dimensions were the same as the standard 275, but the engine was dry-sumped, sheet metal was thinner and many chassis parts were lighter than normal. Author photos.

The 275 GTB as it was introduced in 1964. This was the first Ferrari GT to have cast-alloy wheels. Pininfarina photos.

The 275 GTB introduced in Paris in October 1964, was intended to be a replacement for the Lusso. It was the first Ferrari road car to have all-independent suspension, and the transmission was in unit with the rear axle. Warren Fitzgerald photo.

275 GTB and GTB/C

ENGINE
Type: . . . . Colombo-designed, 60-degree V-12
Bore x stroke, mm/inches: . . . . . 77 x 58.8/3.050 x 2.315
Displacement, cc/cubic inches: 3286/200.5
Valve operation: . . . Single overhead camshaft on each bank
    with roller followers and rocker arms to inclined valves
Compression ratio: 9.2:1
Carburetion: . . . . *Three Weber twin-choke, downdraft
Bhp (Mfr): . . . . 280 @ 7600

CHASSIS & DRIVETRAIN
Clutch: . . . . Single dry-plate
Transmission: . . . Five-speed, all-synchromesh, in unit with
    the differential, all indirect gears
Rear suspension: . . . Independent with unequal-length A-
    arms, coil springs and telescopic shock absorbers
Axle ratio: 3.55:1
Front suspension: . . . Independent with unequal-length A-
    arms, coil springs and telescopic shock absorbers
Frame: . . . . Welded tubular steel, ladder type

GENERAL
Wheelbase, mm/inches: 2400/94.5
Track, front, mm/inches: 1377/54.2
    rear, mm/inches: 1383/54.8
Brakes: . . . . Disc
Tire size, front and rear: . . . Pirelli 210/14 HS or Dunlop 205
    HR/14 SP
Wheels: . . . . Campagnolo alloy
Body builder: . . . . Scaglietti (Pininfarina design)
*The 275 GTB was homologated with three carburetors, but six
Webers were optional. Standard bodies were steel and aluminum, but
all-aluminum bodies were optional, as were Borrani wire wheels.

Interior of the 275 GTB is luxurious, and seats have fore and aft adjustment, but seatback angle is fixed. Ed Niles photo.

At the Frankfurt show in October 1965, the 275 appeared with slight body revisions: the rear deck hinges were outside, the driver's door had no vent window, a hood bulge was added over the carburetors and the nose was slightly longer with a smaller air intake. Pininfarina photo.

A very few, very special 275 GTB's were seen in this configuration. Note the high rear fenders with louvers behind rear wheel opening. Kurt Miska photo.

A 275 GTB (berlinetta) and GTS (spyder) were introduced simultaneously at the Paris show in October 1964. They shared identical chassis and engines, but had completely different bodies.

The 3.3-liter engine was a continuation of the Colombo unit so familiar in Ferraris but, for the first time on a Ferrari road car (and like the 275 GTB), the transmission (a five-speed) was mounted in unit with the rear axle. The clutch was still at the back of the engine, and the driveshaft was supported by a central steady-bearing.

Suspension was independent all around, with concentric coil spring/shock absorbers and unequal-length A-arms. Disc brakes were standard on all four wheels. These were the most sophisticated Ferrari road cars to this date, as Ferrari kept updating and improving his Grand Touring vehicles.

The berlinettas were built by Scaglietti to a Pininfarina design, but the spyders (convertibles to Americans) were all Pininfarina, design and construction. The spyder front was somewhat reminiscent of the earlier 250 GT cabriolets, but the back took the shape of the 330 2+2, modified to suit the new, open body.

The GTS is beautifully finished, and well-detailed, but not all drivers fit the seat/pedals/steering wheel proportions of a Ferrari. The seats are adjustable, with plenty of fore and aft movement, but not enough back rake angle adjustment. Consequently, when the seat is back far enough for a tall driver to be comfortable with the seat-to-pedal distance, the steering is likely to be too far away, and it isn't adjustable.

As a result of moving the transmission to the rear, the GTS has even better balance than most previous Ferraris, and this is apparent in driving ease and handling. In spite of the possibly uncomfortable driving position, fast touring over any type road is safe and enjoyable. It is a neutral-handling car with good road adhesion.

Typical of convertibles, it is noisier than a closed car because you're getting wind and exhaust noise along with engine and drivetrain sounds. The decibel level would be unacceptable to engineers of most car companies, because it wouldn't be acceptable to their customers; but in a Ferrari it doesn't seem to make that much difference, somehow.

In a 1966 road test of the 275 GTS by *Road & Track,* the standing-start quarter mile was covered in 15.7 seconds (top speed, 91 mph) so it was really no faster than the Lusso. But, on a trip through Nevada the engineering editor covered 425 miles in five hours including ''one gas and two lemonade stops'' without fatigue or stress on either car or driver. The ambient air temperature was one hundred degrees Fahrenheit and neither the car's oil or water temperature gauges read higher than normal at any time.

The writer commented about the noise level of the convertible top but felt it wasn't particularly offensive, and was extremely complimentary about the car's behavior on the road. This is the 275 GTB's true element and he was using the car the way it was designed to be used. Excellent suspension and superb brakes allow extremely fast driving with comfort, confidence and safety. And *style*.

Just your typical Ferrari engine compartment. Three downdraft Weber carburetors under a single air cleaner nestled between black crackle-finished valve covers. Scott Malcolm/*Road & Track* photo.

The 275 GTS was introduced at the Paris Salon in October 1964. The body is by Pininfarina, but no crest is shown. Pininfarina photos.

A (removable) hardtop on the 1965 275 GTS. Pininfarina photo.

In 1965, changes were made to the side vents. Parking lights and front bumper over-riders were also added. A removable hardtop was offered but few were made. This is a rare accessory. Pininfarina photo.

275 GTS

ENGINE

Type: . . . . Colombo-designed, 60-degree V-12
Bore x stroke, mm/inches: . . . . . 77 x 58.3/3.050 x 2.315
Displacement, cc/cubic inches: 3286/200.5
Valve operation: . . . Single overhead camshaft on each bank with roller followers and rocker arms to inclined valves
Compression ratio: 9.2:1
Carburetion: . . . . Three Weber twin-choke, downdraft
Bhp (Mfr): . . . . 260 @ 7000

CHASSIS & DRIVETRAIN

Clutch: . . . . Single dry-plate
Transmission: . . . Five-speed, all-synchromesh, in unit with the differential, all indirect gears

Rear suspension: . . . Independent with unequal-length A-arms, coil springs and telescopic shock absorbers
Axle ratio: . . . . 3.30 or 3.55:1
Front suspension: . . . Independent with unequal-length A-arms, coil springs and telescopic shock absorbers
Frame: . . . . Welded tubular steel, ladder type

GENERAL

Wheelbase, mm/inches: 2400/94.5
Track, front, mm/inches: 1377/54.2
rear, mm/inches: 1393/54.8
Brakes: . . . . Disc
Tire size, front and rear: . . . Pirelli 210/14 HS or Dunlop 205 HR/14 SP
Wheels: . . . . Borrani wire, center-lock, knock-off
Body builder: . . . . Pininfarina

Serial Nos. 8329GT-11613GT

Introduced at the Geneva auto show in March 1966, the 330 GTC utilized the chassis of the 275 GTB, the engine of the 330 GT 2+2, and was covered by a Pininfarina body that took the front of the 400 Superamerica and the rear of the 275 GTS. A combination with that many variables could have been a disaster, but the entire car, mechanically and visually, works extremely well.

Even though the basic engine is like that used in the 330 2+2, the cylinder block was redesigned because, unlike the 2+2, the GTC has a rear-mounted transmission which necessitated different mountings for both engine and differential. The driveshaft goes through a torque tube to the transaxle.

Suspension is independent all around, with unequal-length A-arms, coil springs and telescopic shock absorbers; and there are disc brakes on all four wheels.

By this time in Ferrari history, the competition and road models were completely separated, and the new GTC made no pretext of being something it wasn't. What it was, and is, is a super deluxe Grand Touring car which is fast, comfortable and quiet. A good radio could be enjoyed, and air conditioning was an option.

Production of the 330 GTC lasted from mid-1966 to the end of 1968, at which time the engine was enlarged to 4.4 liters, and the car became a 365 GTC. This version was produced through 1969. Visually the two cars were identical except for placement of the engine hot-air outlets which moved from the fender sides to the rear of the hood.

At the Paris Salon in October 1966, a convertible version called the 330 GTS was shown to complement the coupe. Production of the GTS continued alongside the coupe until the end of 1968; at which time it, also, became a 365 GTS, continuing through 1969.

Probably less than two hundred 365 GTC and GTS cars were built in the years they were in production. They were numbered between 11924 and 12795. The 365 engine was identical to that of the 365 2+2 and, in spite of the horsepower increase from 300 to 320, top speed remained the same as the 330, but acceleration was improved.

Other than the enlarged engine displacement, body and chassis specifications were the same as the last 330 GTC and GTS.

A road test of a 330 GTS in *Road & Track* reported that the top had been improved over the 275 GTS because of better sealing around the windows; and the editors were impressed with the ease of putting the top up or down, but they still commented about the wind noise at speed. They were impressed with the seats, both for comfort and adjustment, but weren't happy with the slow electric window lifts that are typical of European-style window mechanisms.

Performance had improved somewhat over the 275 as they recorded 14.9 seconds for the standing-start quarter mile, with a top speed of 95 miles per hour. High praise was given the engine and suspension (improved since its first use on the 275 GTB and GTS), but the disc brakes needed to be warmed up before they performed satisfactorily.

This series, both coupe and convertible, is the epitome of style and class for its time period. These cars have all the Ferrari attributes except that they are elegantly restrained. They are for the person who wants a Ferrari, but doesn't need to tell the world he owns one. Maybe he's a bit smug about his own good taste; he's made it, he knows it, but doesn't care whether anyone else knows it or not.

Introduced at the Geneva auto show in March 1966, the 330 GTC is (in the author's opinion) the best Ferrari road car built. The Pininfarina bodywork is handsome and well finished; it has excellent performance, and with its creature comforts (air conditioning and electric windows were available, and the radio or tape could be heard and appreciated because of the quiet interior) it is a civilized GT car. Author photos.

The 330 GTS is a convertible version of the GTC, with all the same amenities plus a folding top for open-air motoring. It is a bit noisier than the coupe, but is still an excellent GT car. Pininfarina photo.

330 GTC and GTS

ENGINE
Type: . . . . Colombo-based, 60-degree V-12
Bore x stroke, mm/inches: . . . . 77 x 71/3.03 x 2.79
Displacement, cc/cubic inches: 3967/242
Valve operation: . . . Single overhead camshaft on each bank
    with roller followers and rocker arms to inclined valves
Compression ratio: 8.8:1
Carburetion: . . . . Three Weber twin-choke, downdraft
Bhp (Mfr): . . . . 300 @ 7000

CHASSIS & DRIVETRAIN
Clutch: . . . . Single dry-plate
Transmission: . . . Five-speed, all-synchromesh, in unit with
    the differential, all indirect gears
Rear suspension: . . . Independent with unequal-length A-arms, coil springs and telescopic shock absorbers
Axle ratio: 3.44:1
Front suspension: . . . Independent with unequal-length A-arms, coil springs and telescopic shock absorbers
Frame: . . . . Welded tubular steel, ladder type

GENERAL
Wheelbase, mm/inches: 2400/94.5
Track, front, mm/inches: 1401/55.2
      rear, mm/inches: 1417/55.8
Brakes: . . . . Disc
Tire size, front and rear: 205-14
Wheels: . . . . *Campagnolo alloy
Body builder: . . . . Pininfarina
*Borrani wire wheels optional.

Instrument panel of the 330 GTS is virtually identical to the GTC. This one shows air-conditioning outlets in the console, with window lift buttons on either side of the cigarette lighter (bottom) but no radio. Gordon Chittenden/*Road & Track* photo.

Either Campagnolo alloy or Borrani wire wheels were available and the buyer's only other option was open or closed bodywork. Gordon Chittenden/*Road & Track* photos.

Almost exactly two years after the introduction of the 275 GTB, a highly revised edition appeared at the Paris show in 1966. The new car, the 275 GTB/4, looked nearly identical to the 275 GTB, and most mechanical components were the same. The difference was in the engine itself, which was a four-cam V-12. In this form it produced 300 bhp at 8000 rpm.

As in the latest single-cam 275's, the power was transmitted from the engine to the five-speed transaxle via a torque tube. Suspension was still independent all around with the now ubiquitous unequal-length A-arms, concentric tubular shocks with coil springs and disc brakes.

A slight bulge in the hood was the only visual difference between the sohc and dohc versions and, unlike the single-cam, no competition model was forthcoming from Ferrari.

The 275 GTB, in 1964, had been the first Ferrari road car to have all-independent suspension; and this new model was the first Ferrari road car to have a double-overhead-camshaft engine.

At the instigation of Luigi Chinetti, Jr., son of the American Ferrari distributor, a special version of the 275 four-cam was produced in 1967. This was a cabriolet, built by Scaglietti from the basic 275 GTB body shell, and called the NART (for Chinetti's North American Racing Team) Spyder. Less than ten cars were built in this configuration, and all were sold by Chinetti in the U.S.

The NART Spyder is a beautiful car, and one to be coveted by its owners. Approximately 280 of the 275 GTB/4's were built, but I can account for only nine NART Spyders; an exclusivity factor that can't be overlooked.

There was no performance difference between the GTB/4 and GTS/4, and the desirability comes down to personal choice—but as an investment, the open car has to take precedence over the berlinetta.

In a road test of the NART Spyder, *Road & Track* (September 1967 issue) gave the top speed at 155 and the speed at the end of a 14.7-second standing-start quarter mile as 99 miles per hour. I seem to remember Joe Parkhurst's 275 GTB doing the quarter mile at Carlsbad Raceway in a bit over fourteen seconds with a top speed of 102 mph. This was with Joe alone in the car, timed by the raceway's clocks. Most magazine road tests, including the one in *Road & Track* are done with two in the car and assorted test equipment on board. The weight difference could cause the speed difference.

Road & Track went on to praise the brakes, which were outstanding on the 275 but because the discs were larger, increasing the area swept by the brake pads, the GTB/4 brakes were even better.

The 275's don't have the top speed of the later Daytona, but because of their smaller dimensions and lighter weight, they are just as quick in most circumstances. The superb balance and excellent power make them a delight to drive, and there isn't much, if anything, on the road that a 275 GTB/4 driver would have to give way to.

Jean-Pierre Beltoise, the well-known French Grand Prix driver, conducted a road test of a 275 GTB/4 for *l'Auto Journal,* and reported covering forty-six miles in twenty-three minutes on a Sunday afternoon, in spite of "stopping for the tollgates." That's motoring!

The 275 GTB/4 was the first road Ferrari to be powered by a double-overhead-camshaft engine. It was shown for the first time at the 1966 Paris auto show. Strangely, no competition version was built, as with the single-camshaft 275. Ferrari photo.

The 275 GTB/4 was introduced at the Paris show in 1966 (this photo is from the Frankfurt show in 1967). The visual difference between the two-cam and the four-cam was the hood bulge of the 275 GTB/4. Molter photo.

Luigi Chinetti, Jr., conceived the idea for an open version of the GTB/4 and Scaglietti obliged by creating this handsome model called the NART Spyder. Starting with number 09437, nine NART Spyders were built, and all sold in the U.S. Stan Rosenthal/*Road & Track* photos.

---

275 GTB/4 and GTS/4 NART Spyder

ENGINE

Type: . . . . Colombo-based, 60-degree V-12
Bore x stroke, mm/inches: . . . . . . 77 x 58.8/3.050 x 2.315
Displacement, cc/cubic inches: 3286/200.5
Valve operation: . . . Double overhead camshafts on each bank, with cups and spacers operating directly on inclined valves
Compression ratio: 9.2:1
Carburetion: . . . . Six Weber twin-choke, downdraft
Bhp (Mfr): . . . . 300 @ 8000

CHASSIS & DRIVETRAIN

Clutch: . . . . Single dry-plate
Transmission: . . . Five-speed, all-synchromesh, in unit with the differential, all indirect gears

Rear suspension: . . . Independent with unequal-length A-arms, coil springs and telescopic shock absorbers
Axle ratio: 3.55:1
Front suspension: . . . Independent with unequal-length A-arms, coil springs and telescopic shock absorbers
Frame: . . . . Welded tubular steel, ladder type

GENERAL

Wheelbase, mm/inches: 2400/94.5
Track, front, mm/inches: 1401/55.2
rear, mm/inches: 1417/55.8
Brakes: . . . . Disc
Tire size, front and rear: 205-14
Wheels: . . . . Campagnolo alloy
Body builder: . . . . Scaglietti (Pininfarina design)

The 275 GTB/4 (10351) had six Weber carburetors, four overhead camshafts—two per bank—and dry sump lubrication. Author photos.

At the Paris Salon in October 1968, the new Ferrari 365 GTB/4 was displayed. At that time it was the most expensive (at just under $20,000) and fastest (the factory claim of 174 miles per hour was verified in 1970 by a *Road & Track* road test) road car in the company's twenty-one-year history. It also did 107.5 mph at the end of the standing-start quarter mile which was covered in 13.8 seconds.

Like the 275 GTB which preceded it, the 365 had independent suspension—unequal-length A-arms with concentric tubular shock absorbers and coil springs—both front and rear, and Dunlop ventilated disc brakes all around. A welded tubular steel frame tied the two ends together.

The 365 engine was a double-overhead-camshaft V-12, displacing 4.4 liters and, with its six Weber carburetors, produced 352 horsepower at 7500 rpm. Drive went through a five-speed transmission in unit with the differential.

The prototype shown at Paris was designed and built by Pininfarina, but when the Daytona, as the motoring press had dubbed it, went into production a year later, it was once again Scaglietti who built it. And, once again, the bodies were in steel with hood, doors and trunk lid in aluminum.

When driving the Daytona, one gets the feeling that it is heavy; and at 3,600-plus pounds, it is one of the heaviest cars to come from the Ferrari drawing boards—particularly considering it is only a two-place car. But the weight doesn't seem to bother handling, and the excellent horsepower and torque give the Daytona performance to match its looks.

When the Daytona first came out, Ferrari enthusiasts and the motoring press seemed divided about its appearance. Ten years later, those who liked it, love it; and those who didn't like it, do so now. It is an aggressive-looking design that has features later found on many other European cars.

A year after its debut at the Paris show, a convertible version, the 365 GTS/4, was exhibited at the Frankfurt show. Over 1,300 Daytonas were sold, predominantly berlinettas. There are several shops now changing berlinettas into cabriolets for their customers. Some of this comes from a genuine desire to drive an open car, and some of it from the hope that it will increase the value (probably true, but not as much as a factory-built convertible). Open cars have traditionally been more valuable than closed cars, no matter what the make.

The Daytonas were successfully raced, in spite of their weight penalty. Performance, from acceleration to top speed, was excellent, as was handling. The major weakness of the Daytona in competition was its brakes. This was a result of repeated use of the brakes to slow a tremendously fast car (nearly 200 mph at Le Mans in racing trim) that was also heavy. This would not be a problem for road use. What might be a problem to some buyers would be the relatively heavy steering—particularly at slower speeds. I suggest you drive a Daytona in city traffic before putting your money on the line.

As the last of the line of great front-engined V-12 berlinettas, the Daytona holds a special charm for Ferrari enthusiasts. In many ways it is the most 'macho' of all the Ferraris, and its popularity is reflected in its rapidly appreciating price structure. The Daytona is an outstanding automobile, and is one of the most desirable Ferraris.

Unlike other high-performance Ferraris, the Daytona rear was truncated but had no spoiler. Pininfarina photo.

Harrah's 365 GTB/4 was a European version with headlights covered by clear plastic, and equipped with wire wheels at the owner's request. In a 1970 *Road & Track* road test I saw 180 miles per hour indicated at 7000 rpm in fifth gear, which corrected out to 173 mph. Author photos.

365 GTB/4 Daytona

ENGINE

Type: . . . . Colombo-based, 60-degree V-12
Bore x stroke, mm/inches: . . . . 81 x 71/3.19 x 2.79
Displacement, cc/cubic inches: 4390/268
Valve operation: . . . Double overhead camshafts on each bank, with cups and spacers operating directly on inclined valves
Compression ratio: *8.8:1
Carburetion: . . . . Six Weber twin-choke, downdraft
Bhp (Mfr): . . . . *352 @ 7500

CHASSIS & DRIVETRAIN

Clutch: . . . . Single dry-plate
Transmission: . . . Five-speed ZF, all-synchromesh, in unit with the differential, all indirect gears
Rear suspension: . . . Independent with unequal-length A-arms, coil springs and telescopic shock absorbers
Axle ratio: *3.30:1
Front suspension: . . . Independent with unequal-length A-arms, coil springs and telescopic shock absorbers
Frame: . . . . Welded tubular steel, ladder type

GENERAL

Wheelbase, mm/inches: 2400/94.5
Track, front, mm/inches: 1490/58.7
    rear, mm/inches: 1475/58.1
Brakes: . . . . Disc
Tire size, front and rear: *215/70-15
Wheels: . . . . *Cromadora alloy
Body builder: . . . . Scaglietti (Pininfarina design)
*Competition Daytonas had 9.3:1 compression ratio, 405 bhp @ 7500, various axle ratios for different circuits and 10.0/11.0-15 tires. Borrani wire wheels were available on road cars.

The 365 GTB/4 engine was first seen in the U.S. on a stand at the New York auto show in April 1969. The emission equipment on this engine is not on the European version. Author photo.

A convertible version, the 365 GTS/4, made its debut at the Frankfurt auto show in October 1969. Not many were made, and quite a few berlinettas are now being rebuilt into cabriolets. Pininfarina photo.

Posh is the word for the Daytona interior. Unfortunately, the seats have no back adjustment; you have to hope you fit. Hans Tanner photo.

To comply with U.S. law, the Pininfarina-bodied Ferrari 365 GTB/4 now has retracting iodine headlamps, controlled electrically and also manually in case of emergency. The plexiglass band on the older model is replaced by metallic-painted sheeting (probably aluminum). The new car was shown at Geneva. Pininfarina photo.

The 365 GTB/4 Daytona was raced successfully at Daytona, Le Mans, Watkins Glen and the Tour de France; and less successfully at Sebring and Spa-Francorchamps. This is the car (15685) that finished sixth overall and second in class at Le Mans in 1972, sixth overall and first in class at Watkins Glen the same year, and was sixth overall at Daytona in 1976. Author photo.

Filling the engine compartment completely is this European specification 365 four-camshaft engine. The car was Bill Harrah's personal conveyance. Author photo.

After the 365 GTC was phased out, Ferrari was left without a two-place deluxe tourer until a new model, the 365 GTC/4, was shown at the Geneva show in March 1971. This two-place coupe, with body by Pininfarina, actually had two small seats in the back, but Ferrari realistically didn't describe the car as a 2+2.

The chassis had a wheelbase of 98.4 inches, which placed it between the berlinetta and 2+2 in length. Mechanically, it was closer to the berlinetta.

The engine was basically like that of the 365 GTB/4 Daytona, but utilized six sidedraft Weber carburetors feeding into manifolds incorporated in the exhaust cam covers. The resultant engine was considerably wider than the Daytona engine, but was also lower, allowing a low, sloping hood design. More important, it left a large area between the cylinder heads for American anti-pollution equipment. This was the first Ferrari engine created expressly for the U.S. market since stringent controls were placed on emission levels. The five-speed transmission was mounted in unit with the engine.

Enough power was available, even though the American version was slightly detuned from the European non-emission engines (320 and 340 horsepower respectively), to give excellent performance. Once again, though Ferrari brochures quoted weight as 3,190 pounds, a *Road & Track* road test gave weight as 3,825.

Suspension was independent all around with the now common-to-Ferraris unequal-length A-arms and coil springs wound around tubular shock absorbers. Disc brakes were also standard, as was ZF power steering, both of which were necessary for the heavy car.

As the replacement for the 330/365 GTC series, the GTC/4 continued the refinement and luxury that was now expected and received in Ferraris. Air conditioning and a good radio were also included.

In spite of the heavy weight caused by the all-steel body, loads of accessories and generally large dimensions, the '4' was still an excellent road car with the good manners expected of a GT car from Ferrari. The appearance is one of personal taste, I suppose. It's difficult to fault it on a strictly objective level, yet I feel it doesn't have the charisma of, say, one of the berlinettas, a cabriolet or even the previous GTC series.

Regardless, it was, and is, a civilized Grand Touring car in the Ferrari style.

Headlights pop up from compartments above the grille; twin hood vents allow exit of hot air from radiator. Pininfarina photo.

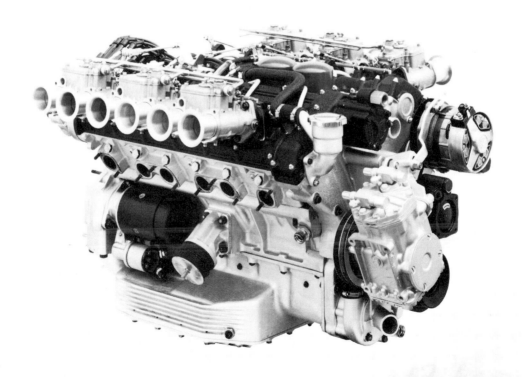

The six sidedraft Webers made the 365 GTC/4 engine lower but wider than the similar unit in the Daytona. This one also has the air-conditioning compressor on the front. Ferrari photo.

Super clean, but not very exciting, lines mark the 365 GTC/4. Large glass area gives excellent visibility. Pininfarina photo.

365 GTC/4

ENGINE
Type: . . . . Colombo-based, 60-degree V-12
Bore x stroke, mm/inches: . . . . 81 x 71/3.19 x 2.79
Displacement, cc/cubic inches: 4390/267.8
Valve operation: . . . Double overhead camshafts on each bank, with cups and spacers operating directly on inclined valves
Compression ratio: 8.8:1
Carburetion: . . . . Six Weber twin-choke, sidedraft
Bhp (Mfr): . . . . 320 @ 6200

CHASSIS & DRIVETRAIN
Clutch: . . . . Single dry-plate
Transmission: . . . Five-speed, all-synchromesh, all indirect gears
Rear suspension: . . . Independent with unequal-length A-arms, coil springs, tubular shock absorbers and anti-roll bar
Axle ratio: 4.09:1
Front suspension: . . . Independent with unequal-length A-arms, coil springs, tubular shock absorbers and anti-roll bar
Frame: . . . . Welded tubular steel

GENERAL
Wheelbase, mm/inches: 2500/98.4
Track, front, mm/inches: 1478/58.2
          rear, mm/inches: 1478/58.2
Brakes: . . . . Disc
Tire size, front and rear: 215/70-15
Wheels: . . . . Cromadora alloy
Body builder: . . . . Pininfarina

Tool kit is shown in trunk compartment that, for Ferrari, is rather spacious. More luggage could be accommodated behind seats. *Road & Track* photo.

Enormous console was dictated by the forward placement of the seats
and the transmission, which is attached to the engine rather than at the
rear axle, as on other contemporary Ferraris. *Road & Track* photo.

Typical of most late-model Ferraris, the 365 GTC/4 could be equipped
with either alloy or these wire wheels. The clean lines are reminiscent
of the Daytona, but the chassis is more like the 365 2+2. Pininfarina
and *Road & Track* photo.

Ferrari's first flat, opposed engine was built in 1964. It was a twelve-cylinder, 1.5-liter Formula 1 engine with 11:1 compression ratio, Lucas fuel injection, and developed 210 horsepower at 11,000 rpm. An opposed engine is often called a 'boxer' engine because of the pistons' reciprocating movement (back and forth, toward and away from each other). The term was originally German, applied to the early VW's and Porsches.

Several other competition Ferraris, both sports and Grand Prix, were built with boxer engines, but the first customer road car with this type of engine was shown at the Turin show in October 1971. It finally went into production in 1973 as the 365 GT4 BB (for 365 Grand Touring, four-cam Berlinetta Boxer). The 4.4-liter engine was mounted behind the driver and ahead of the rear axle; the first mid-engined Ferrari production car. This is discounting the Dino, which wasn't called a Ferrari.

The main body structure was steel, with the front hood, doors and rear deck lid (actually the engine cover) made of aluminum, and the lower body panels constructed of fiberglass. The bodies were assembled in Modena by Scaglietti, and no matter what the main body color, the lower panels were matte black.

Suspension was independent all around; with unequal-length A-arms, coil springs, tubular shock absorbers and anti-roll bars front and rear. The prototype had round- and oval-section steel tubing for the frame, but when the boxer went into production, the frame tubes were square and rectangular in cross section—for easier fabrication.

This engine had two toothed-belt-driven overhead camshafts (also a first for Ferrari) on each bank, with intake ports on the top, and exhaust ports on the lower side. Four, three-throat Weber carburetors fed into twelve ports. The rods and valve gear were interchangeable with the 365 GTC/4.

The boxer's clutch is stiff, and the gated shift lever takes some practice before smooth starts can be made. Acceleration is good but not outstanding (the boxer weighs 3,420 pounds). A road test in 1975 *(Road & Track)* recorded 0-¼ mile in 15.5 seconds with an end-of-quarter speed at 102.5 mph.

Handling is great for the enthusiast driver. The steering, which is heavy at low speeds, lightens up as speed increases and the tail-heavy weight distribution (43/57 percent), which would normally cause oversteer, is offset by a suspension with understeer designed into it—resulting in an agile, maneuverable car.

The boxer isn't as practical as the Daytona. Both passenger accommodation and luggage space suffer, but it is doubtful if any road-going 'customer' Ferrari of the future will have the performance, pizzazz or sheer animal magnetism of the 365 GT4 BB.

The 365 GT4 BB engine marked the first use of a flat, opposed boxer engine in a Ferrari road car. The four overhead camshafts are driven by toothed belts, as on the 308 V-8 engine. Horsepower is 380 at 7200 rpm. Pininfarina photo.

Instrument panel of the 365 GT4 BB is functional, but not as attractive as seen in most Ferraris. The panel is covered with a non-glare material resembling newborn mousehide. Author photo.

365 GT4 BB (Boxer)

ENGINE

Type: . . . . Forghieri-based, flat (opposed) 12
Bore x stroke, mm/inches:. . . . . 81 x 71/3.19 x 2.79
Displacement, cc/cubic inches: 4390/267.8
Valve operation: . . . Double overhead camshafts on each bank, with cups and spacers operating directly on inclined valves
Compression ratio: 8.8:1
Carburetion: . . . . Four Weber three-choke, downdraft
Bhp (Mfr): . . . . 344 @ 7000

CHASSIS & DRIVETRAIN

Clutch:. Single dry-plate
Transmission: . . . . Five-speed, all-synchromesh
Rear suspension: . . . Independent with unequal-length A-arms, coil springs and telescopic shock absorbers
Axle ratio: . . . . 3.90, 3.75 or 3.46:1
Front suspension: . . . Independent with unequal-length A-arms, coil springs and telescopic shock absorbers
Frame:. . . . . Welded tubular steel, with aluminum skin

GENERAL

Wheelbase, mm/inches: 2500/98.4
Track, front, mm/inches: 1500/59.1
    rear, mm/inches: 1510/59.5
Brakes:. . . . . Disc
Tire size, front and rear: 215/70 VR-15
Wheels: . . . . Cromadora alloy
Body builder:. . . . . Scaglietti (Pininfarina design)

Twin air cleaners cover the four Weber three-choke carburetors. Author photo.

If any car looks as though it's going 200 mph while standing still, the Boxer is it. The model isn't a practical touring car, but performance and pizzazz make it all worthwhile. Author photos.

In late 1976, a 512 BB was announced as a replacement for the 365 GT4 BB. Superficially, the two cars looked the same, but closer examination reveals the 'chin spoiler,' or air dam, under the front grille of the 512, NASA ducts on the lower body sides in front of the rear wheel openings, four taillights instead of six, and the rear body length had been increased by four centimeters (about one and a half inches).

Displacement was increased to 4942 cc (up from 4390) by a bore increase of one millimeter and an increase in the stroke of seven millimeters. Horsepower, however, was down from 380 to 360 DIN, but was achieved at 6200 instead of 7000 rpm. With this engine, Ferrari had come back to his Dino-style nomenclature, with 512 representing the five-liter, twelve-cylinder; while the previous boxer was a 365, representing the displacement of one cylinder.

Both the 365 and 512 boxers were raced by private entrants with limited success—primarily because the racing effort was so short-lived that there was no time for progressive development.

The boxers are fantastic cars to drive, with little *raison d'être* other than the sheer pleasure of driving the ultimate sporting GT car. Both passenger and luggage accommodation are minimal, and with the engine just behind the cockpit, the noise is, well, bearable, but not conducive to easy touring.

In other words, you'll get tremendous enjoyment from driving a boxer, but don't plan a trip greater than a few hundred miles if it is necessary to take anything with you other than a traveling companion. And *that* should be someone who enjoys the car as much as you do.

The 512 BB can be distinguished from the 365 GT4 BB by the chin spoiler in front, the NASA air intake on the side and the four taillights at the rear. Pininfarina photo.

512 BB

ENGINE

Type: . . . . Forghieri-based, flat (opposed) 12
Bore x stroke, mm/inches:. . . . . . . 82 x 78/3.23 x 3.07
Displacement, cc/cubic inches: 4942/302.0
Valve operation: . . . Double overhead camshafts on each bank, with cups and spacers operating directly on inclined valves
Compression ratio: 9.2:1
Carburetion: . . . . Four Weber three-choke, downdraft
Bhp (Mfr): . . . . 360 DIN @ 6200

CHASSIS & DRIVETRAIN

Clutch: . . . . Multi disc
Transmission: . . . . Five-speed, all-synchromesh

Rear suspension: . . . Independent with unequal-length A-arms, coil springs and telescopic shock absorbers
Axle ratio: 3.21:1
Front suspension: . . . Independent with unequal-length A-arms, coil springs and telescopic shock absorbers
Frame:. . . . . Welded tubular steel, with aluminum skin

GENERAL

Wheelbase, mm/inches: 2500/98.4
Track, front, mm/inches: 1500/59.1
     rear, mm/inches: 1563/61.5
Brakes:. . . . . Disc
Tire size, front and rear: . . . . . . 215/70 and 225/70 VR-15
Wheels: . . . . Cromadora alloy
Body builder:. . . . . Scaglietti (Pininfarina design)

The 410 Superamerica with Pinin Farina bodywork was introduced to the public at the Brussels auto show in February 1956. The chassis and engine had been seen at the Paris Salon in October 1955.

This series of Ferraris was built in three groups: fifteen cars with serial numbers 0423SA to 0497SA, all on a 110.2-inch wheelbase and all with Pinin Farina bodies except for one Ghia coupe and a coupe and convertible with Boano bodywork; eight more with a 102.3-inch wheelbase and all with Farina bodies, serial numbers 0499SA to 0721SA; and, in 1959, a third series with numbers between 1015SA and 1495SA, still on the 102.3-inch chassis and with Pinin Farina bodies.

Some of the Superamericas looked alike, but all were decidedly custom, one-of-a-kind cars. No two 410's were exactly the same.

The 410's were also big and heavy, as GT cars go. Ferrari specifications are generally pretty accurate, except for weight figures, which seem to be selected in some mysterious way totally unrelated to reality. The 410 supposedly weighed under 3,000 pounds, but a *Road & Track* road test in 1962 gave the curb weight (obtained at a certified public weigh station) as 3,550 pounds.

All this mass is propelled by a powerful engine of 340-400 bhp, depending on whose figures you read, driving through a multiple-disc clutch. The 410 in Harrah's Automobile Collection has been converted to a single dry-plate clutch. This makes the car much easier to drive, but the clutch is unable to handle the torque, and considerable clutch slippage results if the driver is the least bit careless. A four-speed transmission is used on all 410's.

Clutches are probably the weakest link in Ferrari's drivetrain. The standard procedure is to very gently apply throttle pressure as the clutch is released. After the clutch is fully engaged any amount of throttle can be applied without too much fear of slippage. Drag-race starts are not recommended for any Ferrari, and if used will soon destroy the clutch. In spite of a marginal clutch, *Road & Track* achieved a quarter-mile time of 14.6 seconds and 101 mph.

Handling and ride characteristics of the Superamerica reflect its large dimensions and weight, but this will probably be more obvious to someone familiar with other Ferraris than it would be to someone experiencing his first Ferrari drive.

To the knowledgeable Ferrari enthusiast, the Superamerica is ponderous and truck-like—but still a Ferrari. They all have the same feel, the same noises, the same attributes.

The Superamerica was built for cross-country touring, and can cover long distances at high speeds with disconcerting ease. It is a car that is more at home in that environment than in the city or on winding mountain roads where maneuverability is of paramount importance.

Mario Boano built two 410 Superamerica bodies, this coupe (0477) and a similar convertible (0485), in 1956. Boano seemed to be more influenced by Detroit than either Turin or Milan. Moisio/Boano photo.

Two 1956-57 410 Superamericas with very subtle body differences. Visible are the side vent and windshield/side window trim differences. While there is a body builder's crest on each car, only the dark-colored one displays the Pinin Farina name. Pininfarina photos.

The star of the Pinin Farina stand at the 1956 Paris Salon was this 410
Superfast (0483) on the new, shorter chassis. Ralph Poole photo.

0483 was created as a 'showpiece' from the basic 410 SA. A large speedometer and tachometer flanked a dial containing water temperature, fuel and oil pressure gauges. The twin distributors were so far back in the engine compartment that a cowl door had to be opened (behind the hood) to work on them. Ralph Poole photos.

Pinin Farina displayed this 410 Superfast (0719) at Turin in 1957. The basic body shape was similar to the 1956 Superfast (0483), but looked better without the fins. Pininfarina photo.

410 Superamerica I, II and III (SA)

ENGINE
Type:. . . . . Lampredi-designed, 60-degree V-12
Bore x stroke, mm/inches:. . . . . 88 x 68/3.46 x 2.68
Displacement, cc/cubic inches: 4962/302.7
Valve operation: . . . Single overhead camshaft on each bank with roller followers and rocker arms to inclined valves
Compression ratio: *8.5:1
Carburetion: . . . . Three Weber twin-choke, downdraft
Bhp (Mfr): . . . . *340 @ 6000

CHASSIS & DRIVETRAIN
Clutch: . . . . Multiple disc
Transmission: . . . Four-speed, all-synchromesh, direct drive in fourth
Rear suspension: . . . Live axle with semi-elliptic springs, located by parallel trailing arms, and lever-action shock absorbers
Axle ratio:. . . . . *3.67, 3.44, 3.22 or 3.11:1
Front suspension: . . . Independent with unequal-length A-arms, coil springs and lever-action shock absorbers
Frame:. . . . . Welded tubular steel, ladder type

GENERAL
Wheelbase, mm/inches:. *2800/110
Track, front, mm/inches: 1455/58.4
    rear, mm/inches: 1450/58.2
Brakes:. . . . . Aluminum drums with iron liners
Tire size, front and rear: 6.50-16
Wheels: . . . . Borrani wire, center-lock, knock-off
Body builder: . . . . *Pinin Farina
*1958-59 models had 9:1 compression ratio, 400 bhp @ 6500 rpm, 2600 mm wheelbase (102.3 inches) and added axle ratios of 4.85, 4.57, 4.25 3.78, 3.55 and 3.33:1. A few bodies were built by Boano and one was built by Ghia.

Instrument panels varied as much as the exteriors, but this (1477) is fairly typical of the 410 series cars. Author photo.

The trunk of the 1959 410 (1477) is large enough for serious travelers. Author photo.

In 1958 (top) and 1959 (bottom) there were greater differences; top treatment, side vents and headlights being the most noticeable. Pininfarina photos.

The Brussels show was once again, in February 1960, the public debut of a Ferrari Superamerica—this time, the 400 SA. It was a cabriolet by Pinin Farina, with the 'small-block' Colombo V-12 engine in its 95.2-inch wheelbase. Production wasn't to get started until 1961, however.

Like the 410 SA that preceded it, the 400 changed wheelbase in mid-run, but this time it got longer, rather than shorter—from 95.2 to 102.3 inches, in 1962.

Also, like the 410, no two 400's were alike. All but two (built by Scaglietti) carried Pinin Farina bodies, but were individually tailored to customers' wishes. This resulted in a series of cars that were generally the same; basic engine and mechanical specs didn't change through the series, but body design and trim could and did.

The Colombo-designed engine had more displacement than any previous small-block version, with a subsequent increase in horsepower. Claims up to 400 bhp are made and, while we know these 400's were fast, it is doubtful that these customer engines actually produced that much power.

A Superamerica, either 410 or 400, was created for the affluent (even more so than your average Ferrari buyer) automobile enthusiast, the customer who wanted to travel in the best possible style which, to him, meant a Ferrari, but not a run-of-the-mill Ferrari.

All Ferrari road cars of this period had similar chassis; independent front suspension with coil springs, and live rear axle with semi-elliptic springs and parallel trailing arms for axle location.

With their tremendous power, slippery bodywork and heavy weight, these 400 Superamericas needed good brakes. The 400's came with disc brakes, which were far superior to the drum brakes of the 410.

Whereas the 410 had a four-speed transmission, the 400 had a four-speed plus overdrive. Fourth is direct, and overdrive is a step-up ratio of 28.2 percent.

As always, the Pinin Farina bodywork was not only handsome, but well finished. Traveling in a Superamerica was traveling in style. The owners knew it, and all who saw the car knew it, which is what the owners wanted them to know. Isn't that generally the idea of driving something different?

The body design of most Superamericas has worn well, and they still look great, twenty years later.

After the first Superfast (a 410, built in 1956), Pinin Farina displayed Superfast II (on 400 SA chassis number 2207) at Turin in 1960. It had retractable headlights, and no hood scoop. Shortly after, it acquired a hood scoop and vent windows, and the rear skirts were removed. Pininfarina photos.

Pininfarina also built 400 SA cabriolets: one (3309) with covered head-
lights, and the other (2407) with open lights and a removable hardtop.
These cars are, at first glance, much like the 250 GT cabriolets by
Pinin Farina. Pininfarina photos.

400 Superamerica I and II (SA)

ENGINE

Type: . . . . Colombo-designed, 60-degree V-12
Bore x stroke, mm/inches:. . . . . 77 x 71/3.05 x 2.79
Displacement, cc/cubic inches:. 3967/242
Valve operation: . . . Single overhead camshaft on each bank
    with roller followers and rocker arms to inclined valves
Compression ratio: *8.8:1
Carburetion: . . . . *Three Weber twin-choke, downdraft
Bhp (Mfr): . . . . *340 @ 7000

CHASSIS & DRIVETRAIN

Clutch:. . . . . Single dry-plate
Transmission: . . . Four-speed, all-synchromesh, direct drive in
    fourth with electrically-operated overdrive (28.2%) in
    fifth
Rear suspension: . . . Live axle with semi-elliptic springs, lo-
cated by parallel trailing arms, and telescopic shock ab-
sorbers
Axle ratio: . . . . 3.66, 3.78 or 4.00:1
Front suspension: . . . Independent with unequal-length A-
arms, coil springs and telescopic shock absorbers
Frame:. . . . . Welded tubular steel, ladder type

GENERAL

Wheelbase, mm/inches: *2600/102.3
Track, front, mm/inches: 1360/53.5
    rear, mm/inches: 1346/53.0
Brakes:. . . . . Disc
Tire size, front and rear: 6.50-15
Wheels: . . . . Borrani wire, center-lock, knock-off
Body builder: . . . . Pinin Farina
*Early 400 SA's had 9.8:1 compression ratio, 400 bhp @ 6750 rpm
and shorter wheelbase—2413 mm/95.2 inches. A few 400 SA's had
Solex carburetors. Two cars had Scaglietti bodies.

A 400 Superamerica Aerodinamico on the short chassis (probably 3747) is typical of the series, all of which had Pininfarina bodies except for two by Scaglietti. Author photos.

Three 400 Superamericas look similar, but there are differences in grilles, parking-light location, hoods, door handles, and one car has an air outlet behind the rear wheel, in the lower fender. Pininfarina photos.

In 1962, SF II was rebuilt into Superfast IV 400 SA (chassis number 2207). The top configuration was similar, but not identical, to SF III; the retracting headlights had given way to quad lights. This car also underwent a hood change and is shown with and without an air scoop. Pininfarina photos.

More confusion! The engine in this 400 SA (2331) cabriolet has the valve cover configuration of a 410 Lampredi engine, but has removable cylinder heads of the Colombo engine. The car's owner says it is a Colombo engine; it looks like a Lampredi. Paul Swartzel photo.

This 400 SA cabriolet by Pinin Farina appears, with just a casual look, to be a 250 Spyder California, but compare it to the Spyders in Chapter Five. Pininfarina photo.

A 400 SA engine. Karl Dedolph photo.

Superfast III (believed to be chassis number 3361) was shown at Geneva in 1963. It had the same headlight treatment as SF II, but added a thermostatically controlled retracting grille cover. The bodies were very similar, but the top was considerably changed. Pininfarina photo.

Serial Nos. 5951SF-8897SF

Continuing the luxury image Ferrari had established with the 410 and 400 Super-americas, a new king of the road was shown to an admiring public at the Geneva show in March 1964. This new car was called the 500 Superfast.

Its engine was a 4962 cc V-12 and was unique to this model. The design followed the Colombo practice of having removable cylinder heads, but the dimensions were the same as the Lampredi 'long-block' engines of the 410 Superamerica and some of the earlier 250 Europas and 375 Americas.

Other than the engine, mechanical specifications were almost identical to the 330 GT. Drive went through a four-speed transmission, with Laycock de Normanville overdrive, to a live rear axle. Suspension was still independent in front with unequal-length A-arms and coil springs, and the rear axle was supported by semi-elliptic springs and located by parallel trailing arms on each side.

In 1965, the 500 SF underwent running changes that were also being made to the 330 GT 2+2; new engine mounts, suspended pedals and five-speed transmission replaced the four plus overdrive.

Outside, both the 500 SF and 330 GT received new air outlets for the front fenders, but the basic body remained unchanged throughout the model run.

Production started early in 1964 on the 500 Superfast, which bears a strong resemblance to its predecessor, the 400 SA. The main visual differences are uncovered headlights and squared-off tail of the Superfast. Pininfarina photo.

500 Superfast (SF)

ENGINE

Type: . . . . Colombo-based, 60-degree V-12
Bore x stroke, mm/inches:. . . . . 88 x 68/3.46 x 2.68
Displacement, cc/cubic inches: 4962/302.7
Valve operation: . . . Single overhead camshaft on each bank
  with roller followers and rocker arms to inclined valves
Compression ratio:. 8.8:1
Carburetion:. . . . . Three Weber twin-choke, downdraft
Bhp (Mfr):. . . . . 400 @ 6500

CHASSIS & DRIVETRAIN

Clutch: . . . . Multiple-disc
Transmission: . . . *Five-speed, all-synchromesh, direct drive
  in fourth
Rear suspension: . . . Live axle with semi-elliptic springs, located by parallel trailing arms, with telescopic shock

absorbers
Axle ratio:. . . . . . *Various, according to customer's request
Front suspension: . . . Independent with unequal-length A-
  arms, coil springs and telescopic shock absorbers
Frame:. . . . . Welded tubular steel, ladder type

GENERAL

Wheelbase, mm/inches: 2650/104.2
Track, front, mm/inches: 1407/55.5
  rear, mm/inches: 1397/55.2
Brakes:. . . . . Disc
Tire size, front and rear: 6.50-16
Wheels: . . . . Borrani wire, center-lock, knock-off
Body builder:. . . . . Pininfarina
*Virtually all 11 ratios from 410 and 400 SA, and 365 GT 2+2 avail-
able. Four-speed plus overdrive transmission was used in 1964 and
early 1965 models.

Luxurious interiors of the 500 SF are traditional Ferrari/Pininfarina.
The shift lever controls a four-speed, engine-mounted transmission
with electrically-operated O/D. Pininfarina and Karl Dedolph photos.

The 500 Superfast was visually evolutionary from the 400 Superamericas and continued the super-deluxe image of the SA's. The body was almost devoid of decoration, and was totally unprotected from side damage. Pininfarina photo.

The 365 California shared a name with the earlier 250 GT California, but was theoretically a cabriolet successor to the 500 Superfast coupe. The new car was created by the Ferrari/Pininfarina amalgam, which has been so successful over the years, and was unveiled at the 1966 Geneva show.

Power came from a single-overhead-camshaft V-12 similar to that of the 365 P racing engine. The 365 engine in the California had a 4390 cc displacement, 8.8:1 compression ratio and produced 320 horsepower at 6600 rpm. Drive went through a five-speed transmission like that of the 500 SF and the 330 2+2. Power steering was standard and, unlike its contemporaries, Borrani wire wheels were standard and Campagnolo alloy wheels were optional.

During its one year of production, fourteen examples were built, about half of which came to the U.S.

Pininfarina's body design borrowed heavily from other PF designs: the front from the 500 Superfast, and the body sides, with air intake surrounding the door handles, from the 246 Dino. The rear, however, was unique to the 365.

This model is not well known, nor was it well received, I think, because it is so rare. It is big and heavy, in the tradition of the Superamericas, and is classed as one of the 'luxury' Ferrari GT's. But, because it is an open car, it is set apart from most other versions of the Ferrari luxury series.

---

365 California

ENGINE

Type: . . . . Colombo-based, 60-degree V-12
Bore x stroke, mm/inches: . . . . 71 x 71/3.19 x 2.79
Displacement, cc/cubic inches: 4390/268
Valve operation: . . . Single overhead camshaft on each bank with roller followers and rocker arms to inclined valves
Compression ratio: 8.8:1
Carburetion: . . . . Three Weber twin-choke, downdraft
Bhp (Mfr): . . . . 320 @ 6600

CHASSIS & DRIVETRAIN

Clutch: . . . . Single dry-plate
Transmission: . . . Five-speed, all-synchromesh, direct drive in fourth

Rear suspension: . . . Live axle with semi-elliptic springs, located by parallel trailing arms, with telescopic shock absorbers
Axle ratio: 4.25:1
Front suspension: . . . Independent with unequal-length A-arms, coil springs and telescopic shock absorbers
Frame: . . . . Welded tubular steel, ladder type

GENERAL

Wheelbase, mm/inches: 2650/104.2
Track, front, mm/inches: 1397/55.2
    rear, mm/inches: 1389/54.7
Brakes: . . . . Disc
Tire size, front and rear: 205-15
Wheels: . . . . Borrani wire, center-lock, knock-off
Body builder: . . . . Pininfarina

The 365 California's Pininfarina bodywork borrowed its front from the 500 Superfast, and the door handle/air scoop from the 246 Dino. Pop-up driving lights retracted into the nose, just in front of the hood opening. Pininfarina photos.

Several 2+2 bodies were built on Ferrari cars in the early fifties, by Carrozzeria Touring, Ghia and Vignale, but they were not series-built cars, and the rear passenger accommodation was unacceptable for much more than a trip around the block.

The prototype for the first series production Ferrari 2+2 was used as the course marshal's car at the Le Mans 24-Hour Race in June 1960, which was the first time it had been publicly displayed. Its official debut was at the Paris auto show in October 1960, however. This 2+2 was built on the same 102.3-inch wheelbase chassis used for the two-passenger cars, but the engine had been moved forward eight inches to allow for the needed additional passenger space.

The bodywork, by Pinin Farina, was all-new and, with minor changes, continued to the end of 1963 (the start of the replacement 330 2+2) as the 250 GTE.

Mechanically (other than modifications necessary when the engine was moved forward), the 2+2 was almost identical to the two-passenger contemporary Ferraris. It had independent front suspension with coil springs, semi-elliptic rear springs supporting a live axle positioned by twin parallel trailing arms on each side, telescopic shock absorbers and disc brakes all around. The transmission was a four-speed with Laycock de Normanville overdrive.

The cylinder heads were now the standard Ferrari units which followed the Testa Rossa pattern with spark plugs on the outside of the heads, individual intake ports and coil valve springs.

Moving the engine forward was slightly detrimental to handling, as it increased the understeering tendencies. A 2+2 owner was not usually inclined to drive his car as hard as the owner of a two-passenger model, but if he did, the trick was to tweak the steering wheel just a bit going into a corner to break the rear wheels loose, then manage the understeer/oversteer by judicious use of steering and throttle (an easy thing to do with a Ferrari).

This model Ferrari is not one of the most popular, but it is one of the most practical. And in this writer's opinion, one of the least appreciated. The problems solved by Ferrari engineers and Farina designers in transposing the 'Ferrari style' onto a four-passenger car without losing its appeal, were solved beautifully, and successfully.

The 2+2 doesn't have the pizzazz of some other Ferraris, and it isn't any better or any worse mechanically than its contemporaries. But it does offer Grand Touring for a couple with two small children, or four adults can arrive at the theater in grand style without the ladies' clothing being too ruffled.

At the end of the 250 2+2 model run in late 1963, about fifty cars were built (from serial number 4953 to 5175) with a new four-liter—330 V-12—engine. The only identification on this model, to separate it from the 250, is a nameplate on the back that says AMERICA—and not all of them were so labeled. The

330 engine is a Type 209 Ferrari engine, which is several inches longer than the 250 GT engine.

This model, I think, is a sleeper for investment purposes. It won't appreciate as much or as fast as the competition-oriented cars, but it should do better than the normal 250 GTE.

The prototype 250 GTE 2+2, in 1960, had chrome headlight bezels and louvers behind the quarter windows but no louvers on the front fenders. Pininfarina photo.

The second pre-production prototype 250 GT 2+2 had small side reflectors on front fenders, but no louvers. With cleaner side treatment, it is one of the better looking of the series. Pininfarina photo.

The 1961-62 production version had large chrome area around taillights, front parking lights under the headlights and driving lights in front
of grille. Author photos.

250 GTE 2+2

ENGINE

Type: . . . . Colombo-designed, 60-degree V-12
Bore x stroke, mm/inches: . . . . . 73 x 58.8/2.870 x 2.315
Displacement, cc/cubic inches: 2953/180.0
Valve operation: . . . Single overhead camshaft on each bank
    with roller followers and rocker arms to inclined valves
Compression ratio: 8.8:1
Carburetion: . . . . Three Weber twin-choke, downdraft
Bhp (Mfr): . . . . 240 @ 7000

CHASSIS & DRIVETRAIN

Clutch: . . . . Single dry-plate
Transmission: . . . Four-speed, all-synchromesh, direct drive in
    fourth with overdrive in fifth (4.57 axle only)

Rear suspension: . . . Live axle with semi-elliptic springs, lo-
    cated by parallel trailing arms, with telescopic shock
    absorbers
Axle ratio: . . . . 4.57 or 4.25:1
Front suspension: . . . Independent with unequal-length A-
    arms, coil springs and telescopic shock absorbers
Frame: . . . . Welded tubular steel, ladder type

GENERAL

Wheelbase, mm/inches: 2600/102.3
Track, front, mm/inches: 1354/53.3
    rear, mm/inches: 1394/54.9
Brakes: . . . . Disc
Tire size, front and rear: . . . . 6.50-15 or 185-15
Wheels: . . . . Borrani wire, center-lock, knock-off
Body builder: . . . . Pinin Farina

You may think that once you've seen one Ferrari engine compartment, you've seen them all, but there are variations; air cleaner design, location of ancillary components, sometimes even component brands. Author photo.

Late 1962 and 1963 models had chrome headlight rims again, and rearranged parking and driving lights. The taillights were considerably cleaned up as well. Pininfarina photo.

Ferrari holds a press conference early each year in Maranello to display his offerings for the coming year. At his January 1964 press conference, a new four-liter 330 2+2 made its debut and met with decidedly mixed reviews.

The designer/builder was still Pininfarina, but the body was bulbous and, wonder of wonders, had four headlights. The press was enthusiastic while in Ferrari's presence, but once back at their typewriters they were much less so. Griff Borgeson, writing in *Road & Track* (April 1964) quotes bodybuilder Scaglietti on the new 2+2, "We all panic at every new Pininfarina design, convinced that the public will never accept it . . . But watch the 330 and see how the public likes it a few months from now . . . Pininfarina has an uncanny sense for being right about what the public wants . . . As for things that *go,* Ing. Ferrari just keeps on pointing the way."

Apparently both Pininfarina and Scaglietti were right, but in 1965, the model did lose two of its headlights, which brought the shape and style closer to what enthusiasts expected from Ferrari and Pininfarina.

Underneath the metal, the chassis was still all Ferrari in style and substance. The wheelbase was lengthened five centimeters, or about two inches, and the driveline was strengthened to absorb the load of the increased horsepower from the four-liter engine. Koni adjustable shock absorbers were used in conjunction with concentric coil helper springs at the rear, as on the Lusso, and a separate front and rear brake system eliminated the possibility of total brake failure.

Running changes in Ferrari mechanical specifications were incorporated into the 330 2+2 in 1965, such as engine mounting, suspended pedals and making available power steering and air conditioning. Ferrari was truly entering the era of the 'family' or daily 'go-to-work' car.

All bodywork of both the 250 and 330 2+2 was by Pininfarina and should be superior to the two-place cars which are built in smaller quantities, necessitating more handwork. Handwork often covers poor panel contour, or fit, so it looks good on the outside but in actual fact is not as well built as a mass-produced body (it won't stand up as well either).

Alloy disc wheels were standard on 330 2+2's, but wire wheels were optional. Both types have advantages and disadvantages. Wire wheels look better on most Ferrari models, but are difficult to keep clean and have to be checked regularly for bent, broken or loose spokes.

During the four years of production, approximately 1,000 of the 330 2+2's were built, which should make finding one a relatively easy task. Unfortunately, if a 2+2 (250 or 330) needs much engine work, it can be just as costly as redoing a more valuable 250 berlinetta or spyder—either of which are better investments, if that is a major consideration.

The first 330 GT 2+2's were actually 250's with 330 engines and were visually identical. These interim cars were called 330 Americas. Moncalvo photo.

To some observers, the Ferrari prancing stallion became a Percheron
with the advent of the 330 2+2; but what it gave up in looks, it gained
in passenger accommodation. Pininfarina photos.

In 1965, the 330 look changed, with the more classic front featuring two headlights instead of four, and new side vents. At this point, the four-speed O/D transmission gave way to a five-speed; alloy wheels became standard with wire wheels optional; and both power steering and air conditioning were available. Pininfarina photo.

330 GT 2+2

ENGINE
Type: . . . . Colombo-based, 60-degree V-12
Bore x stroke, mm/inches: . . . . 77 x 71/3.03 x 2.79
Displacement, cc/cubic inches: 3967/242
Valve operation: . . . Single overhead camshaft on each bank
   with roller followers and rocker arms to inclined valves
Compression ratio: 8.8:1
Carburetion: . . . . Three Weber twin-choke, downdraft
Bhp (Mfr): . . . . 300 @ 6600

CHASSIS & DRIVETRAIN
Clutch: . . . . Single dry-plate
Transmission: . . . *Four-speed, all-synchromesh, direct drive
   in fourth with electrically operated overdrive (22%) in
   fifth
Rear suspension: . . . Live axle with semi-elliptic springs, lo-
   cated by parallel trailing arms, with telescopic shock
   absorbers
Axle ratio: 4.25:1
Front suspension: . . . Independent with unequal-length A-
   arms, coil springs and telescopic shock absorbers
Frame: . . . . Welded tubular steel, ladder type

GENERAL
Wheelbase, mm/inches: 2650/104.2
Track, front, mm/inches: 1397/55.2
   rear, mm/inches: 1389/54.7
Brakes: . . . . Disc
Tire size, front and rear: 205-15
Wheels: . . . . *Borrani wire, center-lock, knock-off
Body builder: . . . . Pininfarina
*1966-67 2+2's had five-speed transmissions. In 1965 alloy wheels
became standard and wire wheels were optional.

More than 2,000 of the 250 and 330 GT 2+2's had been produced by Ferrari/Pininfarina in the eight years of their model run, attesting to the desirability of the body style. Buyers of this body type were generally more concerned about creature comforts and space than were the buyers of the two-passenger models, and Ferrari introduced more and more features calculated to attract this buyer.

A new 2+2 was unveiled at the Paris Salon in October 1967, and displayed mechanical features previously not seen on production Ferraris. The new model had full independent suspension (the first 2+2 to be so equipped), concentric Koni telescopic shock absorbers and coil springs all around, coupled with a Koni and Ferrari-developed self-leveling rear suspension. Power steering and air conditioning were standard equipment.

The chassis was still the typical Ferrari welded-tube arrangement but with the advent of independent rear suspension, drive went through the single disc dry-plate clutch and five-speed, all-synchromesh transmission to the rear axle assembly via a torque tube. This setup was already in use in the 330 GTC and 275 GTB/4; one advantage being that less noise was transmitted to the interior.

Wheelbase of the 365 2+2 was 2650 mm (104.3 inches), as on the 330 2+2; but the body had an entirely new look, more reminiscent of the Superfast than of the previous 2+2's. The 365 clearly had the most effort put into convenience features of any Ferrari to date, and with the best results.

The 365 2+2 is big, and heavy, when compared to GT cars of the world, but because of its Ferrari heritage it retains as many of the traditional sporting characteristics as possible.

Some Ferrari historians and researchers will no doubt quarrel with my three-star rating of this car when the two previous 2+2's got only two stars. My reason for this is simply that the 365 was the most sophisticated, most up-to-date state-of-the-art Ferrari produced up to its date of manufacture. It will come closer to giving its passengers a ride quality and comfort level compatible to the eighties than will any of the older model Ferraris—without losing the 'Ferrari feel.'

The 365 GT 2+2 introduced in 1967 was the first Ferrari 2+2 to have all-independent suspension. It was also the first Ferrari to have a self-leveling rear suspension. Pininfarina photos.

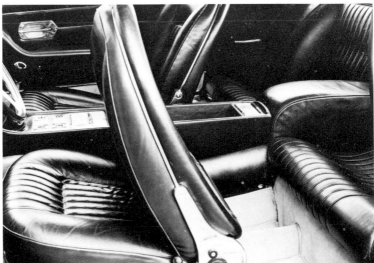

Luxurious interior is extremely comfortable for front seat passengers, with plenty of seat travel and back angle adjustment, but when rear passengers are carried, it gets tight. Pininfarina/Hans Tanner photos.

Alloy wheels were standard on the 365 2+2, but Borrani wire wheels were optional for the 'traditionalist' Ferrari buyer. *Road & Track* photo.

A larger engine and 2+2 bodywork squeezed the engine even tighter into its compartment. The addition of air conditioning and power steering further complicated the available space. Coltrin photo.

365 GT 2+2	
ENGINE	
Type:	Colombo-based, 60-degree V-12
Bore x stroke, mm/inches:	81 x 71/3.19 x 2.79
Displacement, cc/cubic inches:	4390/268
Valve operation:	Single overhead camshaft on each bank with roller followers and rocker arms to inclined valves
Compression ratio:	8.8:1
Carburetion:	Three Weber twin-choke, downdraft
Bhp (Mfr):	320 @ 6600
CHASSIS & DRIVETRAIN	
Clutch:	Single dry-plate
Transmission:	Five-speed, all-synchromesh, direct drive in fourth
Rear suspension:	Independent with unequal-length A-arms, coil springs, and telescopic shock absorbers (with hydro-pneumatic leveling device)
Axle ratio:	4.25:1
Front suspension:	Independent with unequal-length A-arms, coil springs and telescopic shock absorbers
Frame:	Welded tubular steel, ladder type
GENERAL	
Wheelbase, mm/inches:	2650/104.2
Track, front, mm/inches:	1437/56.6
rear, mm/inches:	1468/57.8
Brakes:	Disc
Tire size, front and rear:	215/70 VR-15
Wheels:	°Cromadora alloy
Body builder:	Pininfarina
°Wire wheels optional.	

In European terminology, the 365 GT4 2+2 is a coupe, but Americans would more likely refer to it as a two-door sedan, because of its general appearance and interior accommodation. Its wheelbase is two inches longer, but its overall length is seven and one half inches shorter than the 365 2+2 which preceded it.

When this new 2+2 was introduced at the Paris show in 1972, a year and a half had elapsed since production stopped on the 365 2+2, which is unusual for Ferrari; he usually has a replacement ready to go into production before the previous model is dropped.

Mechanically, the new car, the 365 GT4, was like the 365 GTC/4 rather than the 2+2 it was replacing. A four-cam, 4.4-liter V-12 with six horizontal Weber carburetors furnished the power, which went through a five-speed transmission and torque tube to the chassis-mounted differential.

Ferrari specifications, while always interesting and impressive, tend to be similar from model to model (at least for contemporary models from the company), so the main interest in this new 2+2 was in the Farina bodywork.

It was not only on a longer wheelbase and yet shorter overall than its predecessor, but passenger and luggage space had also been enlarged considerably. ''Smaller on the outside, larger on the inside'' had genuine meaning.

In 1975 I had the pleasure of driving Bill Harrah's personal 365 GT4 from Reno, Nevada, to Monterey, California (for the Historic Car Races and Pebble Beach Concours d'Elegance), and return. The car is heavy. You can tell it by the general feel of the controls and response, but it didn't seem to detract from performance, and I know it didn't detract from my enjoyment of the car.

We had more than enough room for two and luggage, and it proved to be comfortable, no matter what the road surface or driving conditions (during the trip we started from the 4,500 feet altitude of Reno, went up to 9,000 feet at the top of Mt. Rose Highway, and back down to sea level at Monterey).

I kept to legal speed limits most of the time, but found that the car could crest the top of Mt. Rose Highway at 90 mph; and this at nearly 9,000 feet altitude, going uphill, on a mildly winding road. Given a straight road I think the car could easily have topped 100 mph at the summit of the mountain.

This test was unnecessary, of course (don't write me a letter about it), but was a lot of fun, and more than satisfied any question I might have had about the performance of a car that Ferrari enthusiasts think has been emasculated.

The 365 GT4 2+2 was introduced in 1972 as a replacement for the
365 2+2, but mechanically it was like the 365 GTC/4, with a 20-centi-
meter-longer wheelbase. Pininfarina photo.

365 GT4 2+2

ENGINE

Type: . . . . Colombo-based, 60-degree V-12
Bore x stroke, mm/inches: . . . . 81 x 71/3.19 x 2.79
Displacement, cc/cubic inches: 4390/267.8
Valve operation: . . . Double overhead camshafts on each
    bank, with cups and spacers operating directly on in-
    clined valves
Compression ratio: 8.8:1
Carburetion: . . . . Six Weber twin-choke, sidedraft
Bhp (Mfr): . . . . 320 @ 6200

CHASSIS & DRIVETRAIN

Clutch: . . . . Single dry-plate
Transmission: . . . Five-speed, all-synchromesh, direct drive in
    fourth
Rear suspension: . . . Independent with unequal-length A-
arms, coil springs, tubular shock absorbers and anti-roll
bar
Axle ratio: 4.09:1
Front suspension: . . . Independent with unequal-length A-
arms, coil springs, tubular shock absorbers and anti-roll
bar
Frame: . . . . Welded tubular steel

GENERAL

Wheelbase, mm/inches: 2700/106.3
Track, front, mm/inches: 1470/57.9
    rear, mm/inches: 1500/59
Brakes: . . . . Disc
Tire size, front and rear: 215/70-15
Wheels: . . . . Cromadora alloy
Body builder: . . . . Pininfarina

Serial Nos. 27001-

Those who thought Ferrari had deserted the sports and GT markets when he added power steering and air conditioning as standard equipment on some models were really in for a shock when the 1976 Paris show previewed a Ferrari equipped with an automatic transmission.

The car is basically the same as the previous 365 GT4 2+2, with the engine enlarged to 4823 cc. It comes in two versions: the 400 GT, with a five-speed manually shifted transmission; and the 400 A, with a turbo Hydra-matic three-speed automatic transmission.

The transmission is furnished by General Motors, and recalibrated to fit the torque characteristics of the V-12. The five-speed manual is made by Ferrari.

Pininfarina had also done further work to add comfort and convenience to the interior—redesigned seats, for example. The front seats slid forward on their tracks when the seatback was tilted forward (to allow more room for backseat passengers to get in or out) and were of a new shape that gave more comfort. A quadraphonic stereo system was made a part of the radio/tape system.

Outside, a small spoiler was now incorporated into the lower part of the front end, the taillights were redesigned, a remote-control outside mirror was attached to the driver's door, and the Cromadora wheels were now attached by five lug nuts instead of the center-lock knock-off hubs used before.

Neither this, nor the previous version, was made for U.S. sales, because Ferrari had decided to concentrate on the V-8 as his 'Americanized' Ferrari—and it's a pity. Unfortunately, it isn't in Ferrari's best interests to build them for the very limited U.S. market.

You could buy a 365 GT4 2+2 in Europe and run it through one of the U.S. shops that legalize imported cars, but it would cost nearly $100,000 by the time it was certified. You'd have a great car, though, even compared to Ferraris or other exotic cars.

While Walter Mitty might imagine himself (in one of the earlier Ferraris) as Taruffi in the Mille Miglia, or Gendebien in the Tour de France, there is no mistaking the Rodeo Drive or Park Avenue feeling of the 400 GT or 400 A. The historic V-12 engine sound is there—muffled by insulation and, if converted to U.S. specs, by emission equipment—but the luxurious interior with its air conditioning and stereo sound system leave no doubt about the purpose of this model.

The available power and the excellent suspension will allow high-speed touring in great comfort and with a feeling (real) of safety, but it isn't the Ferrari of old that asked to be driven hard on a winding road while chasing or being chased by Porsches and Cobras.

It is a Ferrari for those of us who now put creature comforts and style ahead of power and speed, without really sacrificing all of the latter.

The interior, like the mechanical components, is very reminiscent of the 365 GTC/4, but the 400 has room for two genuine seats in the back. Slight differences can be noted between the manual-shift 365 and the 400 Automatic interiors. Pininfarina photos.

Introduced in 1976, the 400 GT and 400 Automatic shared the same mechanical and body configuration as the 365 GT4, but now with a small spoiler and bolt-on star-design alloy wheels. Pininfarina photo.

400 GT and 400 Automatic

ENGINE

Type: . . . . Colombo-based, 60-degree V-12
Bore x stroke, mm/inches: . . . . 81 x 77/3.19 x 3.05
Displacement, cc/cubic inches: 4823/294.2
Valve operation: . . . Double overhead camshafts on each bank, with cups and spacers operating directly on inclined valves
Compression ratio: 8.8:1
Carburetion: . . . . Six Weber twin-choke, sidedraft
Bhp (Mfr): . . . . 340 @ 6500

CHASSIS & DRIVETRAIN

Clutch: . . . . *Single dry-plate
Transmission: . . . *Five-speed, all-synchromesh, direct drive in fourth
Rear suspension: . . . Independent with unequal-length A-arms, coil springs, tubular shock absorbers and anti-roll bar
Axle ratio: *4.30:1
Front suspension: . . . Independent with unequal-length A-arms, coil springs, tubular shock absorbers and anti-roll bar
Frame: . . . . Welded tubular steel

GENERAL

Wheelbase, mm/inches: 2700/106.3
Track, front, mm/inches: 1470/57.9
        rear, mm/inches: 1500/59
Brakes: . . . . Disc
Tire size, front and rear: 215/70-15
Wheels: . . . . Cromadora alloy
Body builder: . . . . Pininfarina
*400 A has GM Turbo 400 three-speed automatic and 3.25:1 axle ratio.

On the Pininfarina stand at the 1965 Paris auto show appeared a vehicle labeled Dino 206 S Speciale. Its engine was a Ferrari design; double-overhead-camshaft V-6 with sixty-five degrees between the cylinder banks, and the engine mounted just behind the driver. It was a styling exercise built on a racing chassis (serial number 0834). The engine was a facade, with no internal working parts.

A year later, at the Turin show, a working prototype appeared, called the Dino Berlinetta GT. This was a running automobile but was not to be a production car—yet. Exactly a year later, at Turin again, the car that was to become the 246 Dino GT was shown for the first time. It retained the V-6 dohc engine, but the engine was mounted transversely just ahead of the rear axle.

At this point, the engine was still a two-liter V-6 which was built by Fiat and installed in the Ferrari-designed chassis. Scaglietti was responsible for the construction (Farina design, again) after the chassis was received from Ferrari and the engine from Fiat. The car was called a Dino, and there was no Ferrari emblem or nameplate anywhere on the car.

The vast majority of 206 Dinos, about one hundred in all, were sold in Europe. The 246 version was announced early in 1969, but went into production at the end of 1969. These are the cars you'll most likely find in the U.S.

Visually, the 206/246 Dinos remained pretty much the same throughout the model run; but in 1970 the center-lock knock-off hubs gave way to the five-bolt wheels, and in 1972 a GTS body style (with removable roof panel, which stowed behind the seats over the passenger compartment) was introduced.

If you intend to purchase a 206 or 246 Dino, one of the first things you should do is have a competent mechanic check the tension of the timing chain on the forward bank of cylinders (remember this is a transverse-mounted engine). It has been all too common for lazy mechanics to overlook the necessary retensioning of the chain during service, with the result that a chain will occasionally stretch to the point where it slips a tooth on the sprocket. This can be disastrous to the forward cylinder head.

These are quick, maneuverable cars which are enjoyable to drive. They don't have the brute power or marvelous sounds of the V-12 Ferraris, but on a tight, winding road situation they are the match for almost anything on wheels, because their inherent balance makes up for a lack of horsepower.

The Dino is also an excellent car for city driving, because of its light steering and quick response to control input, but the driver's vision is not good to the sides or rear.

The fact that Dinos were not advertised or sold as Ferraris shouldn't detract from their value as an enthusiast's car. They were sold by Ferrari dealers, and I doubt that the lack of a Ferrari emblem or nameplate kept salesmen from calling them Ferraris. And I bet you'll pay Ferrari prices to get work done on a 246 Dino, but there are fewer parts to buy.

The Dino V-6 engine, mounted transversely, just forward of the rear axle assembly, is built mainly by Fiat; except for the lower section (containing oil sump, transmission, differential and driveshafts) which is built by Ferrari. *Road & Track* photo.

The Dino 206 GT was first shown in 1967 and was produced for European sale. Few found their way to the U.S. No 206 or 246 Dino carried a Ferrari nameplate, and it wasn't until the 308 Dino that the series was given Ferrari insignia. Pininfarina photo.

The Dino 246 GT was a 1969 replacement for the 206 Dino. The car shown is a 1969 model with the knock-off hubs, which were phased out early in 1970. Pininfarina photo.

The instruments are different, but the panel layout of the 246 Dino is identical to the Daytona. *Road & Track* photo.

246 GT and GTS Dino

ENGINE

Type: . . . . Rocchi-designed, 65-degree V-6
Bore x stroke, mm/inches: . . . . . . 92.5 x 60.0/3.64 x 2.36
Displacement, cc/cubic inches: 2418/145
Valve operation: . . . Double overhead camshafts on each bank, with cups and spacers operating directly on inclined valves
Compression ratio: 9.0:1
Carburetion: . . . . Three Weber twin-choke, downdraft
Bhp (Mfr): . . . . 175 @ 7000

CHASSIS & DRIVETRAIN

Clutch: . . . . Single dry-plate
Transmission: . . . Five-speed, all-synchromesh, all-indirect
Rear suspension: . . . Independent with unequal-length A-arms, coil springs, tubular shock absorbers and anti-roll bar
Axle ratio: 3.62:1
Front suspension: . . . Independent with unequal-length A-arms, coil springs, tubular shock absorbers and anti-roll bar
Frame: . . . . Welded tubular steel

GENERAL

Wheelbase, mm/inches: 2336/92.1
Track, front, mm/inches: 1427/56.2
rear, mm/inches: 1430/56.3
Brakes: . . . . Disc
Tire size, front and rear: 205/70 VR-14
Wheels: . . . . Cromadora alloy
Body builder: . . . . Scaglietti (Pininfarina design)

The 246 GTS Dino was introduced in 1972. It shared the mechanical specifications and basic body of the GTB, but notable differences can be seen in the tops. Pininfarina photos.

The Paris Salon of 1973 was, as had happened so many times before, the occasion of a Ferrari debut. And, again, there were some firsts for the make. The new car had a transverse-mounted, double-overhead-camshaft V-8 mounted just ahead of the rear axle, and the bodywork was by Bertone. This was the first non-Farina-designed Ferrari GT production car in nearly twenty years.

The new car was designed as a 2+2, even though it didn't carry that designation in its specification. And it had a Dino insignia on the front with no Ferrari prancing horse emblem in evidence anywhere.

Bertone's task was difficult. Designing a 2+2 with a mid engine has to be a tremendous challenge. The styling of the 308 GT4 hasn't won large acclaim, but considering the design problems, the solution is quite good.

All independent suspension was used with unequal-length A-arms and coil springs, and ventilated disc brakes were now the standard Ferrari equipment.

The engine had ninety degrees between cylinder banks, four Weber downdraft carburetors and, with 8.8:1 compression ratio, produced 205 horsepower at 7700 rpm. Unlike the 246 Dino, the engine was produced entirely by Ferrari.

The Bertone bodywork has continued basically unchanged, but in late 1976, the Ferrari prancing horse appeared on the nose, the wheel hubs and the steering wheel center. No explanation was given for the sudden change, but it is felt that Ferrari finally decided the car was worthy of the Ferrari name.

In view of the varied engine configurations used by Ferrari since 1947—in-line four and six, 60-, 65- and 120-degree V-6, V-8, V-12, flat eight and flat twelve—the 246 Dino should also have been called a Ferrari. Perhaps the Dino name was being continued as a tribute to Enzo Ferrari's late son Alfredo 'Dino' Ferrari, who has been given credit for instigating the V-6-engined competition cars that also bear his name.

The 308 GT4 is not a luxurious 2+2 because of its limited space, but like many 2+2's before it, is quite satisfactory for short, around-town use for four persons. It would only be suitable for travel for two plus luggage, however.

Because the 308 GT4 isn't as popular as the two-passenger models of various types, it should still be a relatively good buy. It is questionable whether it will ever appreciate as much as its brethren, but it is still a Ferrari.

The Dino 308 V-8 engine is built entirely by Ferrari and broke new ground by having toothed-belt-driven camshafts, rather than chains, which drive the cams on all Ferrari V-12's (the flat-twelve Boxer shares the toothed-belt-drive system). As in the 246, the 308 Dino is mounted transversely just ahead of the rear axle. Ferrari photo.

Although designed as a 2+2, this example is set up for 2+luggage. Bertone photo.

308 GT4

ENGINE

Type: . . . . Rocchi-designed, 90-degree V-8
Bore x stroke, mm/inches: . . . . 81 x 71/3.19 x 2.79
Displacement, cc/cubic inches: 2927/179
Valve operation: . . . Double overhead camshafts on each bank, with cups and spacers operating directly on inclined valves
Compression ratio: 8.8:1
Carburetion: . . . . Four Weber twin-choke, downdraft
Bhp (Mfr): . . . . *205 @ 6600

CHASSIS & DRIVETRAIN

Clutch: . . . . Single dry-plate
Transmission: . . . Five-speed, all-synchromesh, all-indirect
Rear suspension: . . . Independent with unequal-length A-arms, coil springs, tubular shock absorbers and anti-roll bar
Axle ratio: 3.71:1
Front suspension: . . . Independent with unequal-length A-arms, coil springs, tubular shock absorbers and anti-roll bar
Frame: . . . . Welded tubular steel

GENERAL

Wheelbase, mm/inches: 2550/100.4
Track, front, mm/inches: 1460/57.5
rear, mm/inches: 1460/57.5
Brakes: . . . . Disc
Tire size, front and rear: 205/70 VR-14
Wheels: . . . . Cromadora alloy
Body builder: . . . . Bertone
*One factory brochure lists 205 @ 6600, but another brochure says 240 @ 6600. Both list the European GT4 at 255 bhp.

The Dino 308 GT4 was first shown at the Paris Salon in 1973, and established a number of firsts for Ferrari; his first mid-engined 2+2 (and a V-8, mounted transversely, at that), and his first production car with bodywork by Bertone. Bertone photo.

At the Paris Salon in October 1975, there was (again) a new Ferrari making its public debut. This was a sleek, two-place, mid-engined design by (again) Pininfarina. When the 308 GTB went into production, it was (again) made by Scaglietti.

Utilizing the best design features of the 246 Dino and the 365 GT BB, the new 308 GTB was a handsome styling exercise, destined to be the Ferrari of the 1980's—for the U.S. market, at least.

The first 308 GTB bodies were part metal, but mostly fiberglass—the first such use of this material for a Ferrari road car (some of the single-seat racing cars had used fiberglass), but subsequent production models were all metal. Even though the fiberglass was of excellent finish, Ferrari customers were not mentally adjusted to accept 'their' cars in plastic.

The four-cam, ninety-degree V-8 engine was mounted transversely just ahead of the rear axle. Camshaft drive was by toothed belts, and carburetion was by four, twin-choke downdraft Webers. Engine output was rated at 255 bhp at 7700 rpm, and drove through a five-speed transmission.

Suspension was all independent, with the now-familiar unequal-length A-arms front and rear, with coil springs and disc brakes all around. Wheels were Cromadora alloy with five-bolt attachment.

In 1977, an open version, the 308 GTS, was shown at the Frankfurt show. The GTS was a Targa-type spyder with only the small section over the seats being removable. This panel stowed behind the seats when removed from the roof section. Both the open and closed cars carried the Ferrari prancing horse emblems, and were officially Ferrari Dinos, rather than simply Dinos as were the 246's.

For 1981, Bosch K-Jetronic fuel injection was added, and the car became the 308 GTBi.

Old Ferrari hands decry the descent from a V-12 to a V-8 for power, but the 308 is a Ferrari through and through, regardless of the sounds from the exhaust.

Performance is outstanding, even with all the emission controls necessary for U.S. sale, and handling is exemplary. Controls are stiff at low speeds, but get lighter as speed increases, the brakes are excellent and the driver always feels completely in control.

The shift gate is notchy, but positive, and the clutch/throttle interplay is easily learned. Vision isn't great—in fact, it leaves a lot to be desired for in-town driving. On the road, though, where the main concern is what's in front of you, the view ahead is fine.

The 308 GTB, or GTS, is a car to be enjoyed, but not necessarily one in which to travel cross-country. Luggage space is very minimal, with a bit in front with the spare tire, and space behind the engine for larger pieces. This area, however, gets pretty warm.

Full complement of instruments and lights, including warnings for the catalytic converters getting too hot, face the driver in the small and crowded instrument cluster. Author photo.

Paris once again hosted, in 1975, the debut of an important Ferrari model, the Dino 308 GTB. The first series of cars has fiberglass bodies, but later models were all metal. In both cases, the bodywork was by Scaglietti to Pininfarina design. Ferrari photo.

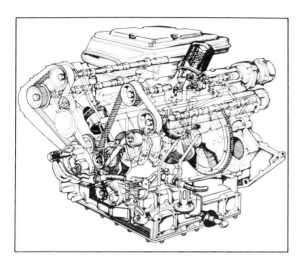

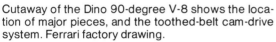

Cutaway of the Dino 90-degree V-8 shows the location of major pieces, and the toothed-belt cam-drive system. Ferrari factory drawing.

Getting in or out of a 308 requires a certain amount of personal flexibility; but once seated, it's obvious that the car was designed for enthusiast drivers. Panel under right side of dash covers the fuse panels. Author photo.

308 GTB and GTS

ENGINE
Type: . . . . Rocchi-designed, 90-degree V-8
Bore x stroke, mm/inches: . . . . 81 x 71/3.19 x 2.79
Displacement, cc/cubic inches: 2927/179
Valve operation: . . . Double overhead camshafts on each bank, with cups and spacers operating directly on inclined valves
Compression ratio: 8.8:1
Carburetion: . . . . *Four Weber twin-choke, downdraft
Bhp (Mfr): . . . . *205 @ 6600

CHASSIS & DRIVETRAIN
Clutch: . . . . Single dry-plate
Transmission: . . . Five-speed, all-synchromesh, all-indirect
Rear suspension: . . . Independent with unequal-length A-arms, coil springs, tubular shock absorbers and anti-roll bar
Axle ratio: 3.71:1
Front suspension: . . . Independent with unequal-length A-arms, coil springs, tubular shock absorbers and anti-roll bar
Frame: . . . . Welded tubular steel

GENERAL
Wheelbase, mm/inches: 2340/92.1
Track, front, mm/inches: 1460/57.5
        rear, mm/inches: 1460/57.5
Brakes: . . . . Disc
Tire size, front and rear: 205/70 VR-14
Wheels: . . . . Cromadora alloy
Body builder: . . . . Scaglietti (Pininfarina design)
*Bosch K-Jetronic fuel injection for 1981 (308 GTBi & 308 GTSi).
Factory brochures list horsepower variously as 205 or 240.

Engine access is not the best, and luggage is placed behind the engine, under a zippered cover, and it is not suggested that you carry anything in this compartment that would be affected by engine heat (chocolate bars, for example). Author photo.

In 1977, the GTS joined the ranks, sharing the GTB's bodywork but with black louvers covering the glass behind the doors, and a removable top section that stowed behind the seats. The look has remained the same and this car is a 1981 308 GTSi. Author photos.

The latest in a long line of exciting Grand Touring cars from Ferrari made its debut at the Geneva auto show in March 1980. It is the 2+2 Mondial 8, with Pininfarina bodywork. The Mondial name (pronounced Mōhn dē ăhl´) was used by Ferrari way back in the early fifties for a two-liter dohc, four-cylinder sports/racing car—also carrying Pinin Farina bodywork.

The Mondial has its three-liter V-8 mounted transversely behind the rear seat, as in the Bertone-bodied 308 GT4. The wheelbase has been lengthened by almost four inches and the seats redesigned so passengers have not only more room, but more comfortable seats as well.

In addition to the normal instruments one expects to find in a high-performance GT car, Ferrari has added electronic monitoring for fluid levels, doors ajar and lights. The interior is upholstered in Connolly leather, the leather-covered steering wheel is adjustable for height and reach. Air conditioning and central locking for all doors are standard equipment, as are the remote-control outside rearview mirror and the electric radio antenna. An electrically operated sun roof is optional.

The Mondial 8 has to be the most technically innovative model to come from Ferrari. Its success remains to be seen, but the necessary ingredients are all there. It has not been certified for U.S. sale, as this is written in early 1981, but the very conception of the Mondial 8 would point it toward the American market.

Mondial 8

ENGINE
Type: . . . . Rocchi-designed, 90-degree V-8
Bore x stroke, mm/inches:. . . . . . . 81 x 71/3.19 x 2.79
Displacement, cc/cubic inches:. 2927/179
Valve operation: . . . Double overhead camshafts on each bank, with cups and spacers operating directly on inclined valves
Compression ratio:. 8.8:1
Carburetion: . . . . Bosch K-Jetronic fuel injection
Bhp (Mfr):. . . . . 205 @ 6600

CHASSIS & DRIVETRAIN
Clutch:. . . . . Single dry-plate
Transmission: . . . Five-speed, all-synchromesh, all-indirect
Rear suspension: . . . Independent with unequal-length A-arms, coil springs, tubular shock absorbers and anti-roll bar
Axle ratio: 4.06:1
Front suspension: . . . Independent with unequal-length A-arms, coil springs, tubular shock absorbers and anti-roll bar
Frame:. . . . . Welded tubular steel

GENERAL
Wheelbase, mm/inches: 2650/104.2
Track, front, mm/inches: 1495/58.9
        rear, mm/inches: 1517/59.8
Brakes:. . . . . Disc
Tire size, front and rear: . . . . 240/55 VR 390
Wheels: . . . . Cromadora alloy
Body builder:. . . . . Pininfarina

Pininfarina's design of the new Mondial 8 was first seen at the 1980 Geneva auto show. Production was scheduled to start in 1981. Pininfarina photos.

THE RARE AND EXOTIC

The Ferraris covered in the front part of this book are the ones you'll most likely be able to find for sale, and the ones that will be obtainable without spending more than you'd pay for a good house. The cars pictured in this section are rare, and expensive. They will not usually be listed in classified ads or, generally, show up at auctions. Word of the availability of one of these rare gems travels in rather close-knit circles and you have to be 'in' to be part of the grapevine.

So how do you get 'in?' Join one or all of the Ferrari clubs and get to know the members who already have one or more of the exotics, and subscribe to the *Ferrari Market Letter.* If you're honest about it, and don't make a fool of yourself, sooner or later you'll get firsthand information about a car that you might want. Hopefully, by that time, you'll also be knowledgeable enough (or have several informed friends who can help) to correctly evaluate a car when the opportunity does come.

Buying the right Ferrari can be a marvelous experience, both emotionally and financially. Buying the wrong one can be a disaster. There's no way I can tell you that a certain car is the wrong one; the one that's right for you may be the wrong one for somebody else, and vice versa.

But go to it, you'll enjoy looking, anyway.

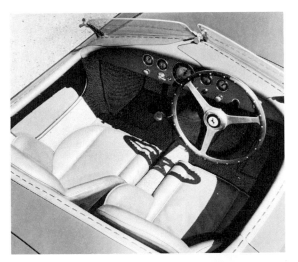

The Ferrari that brought attention to the marque in America was the 166 MM (Mille Miglia). It had a two-liter V-12 engine and five-speed unsynchronized transmission and was based on the Grand Prix Ferrari (note the cylindrical fuel tank, just ahead of the spare tire, which had to fit inside the single-seat body). This model was called the 'barchetta' or 'little boat.' The car shown is 0004M, which is in Harrah's Automobile Collection in Reno, Nevada. Author photos.

The 375 MM—this one is 0322AM—is one of the hairiest, most intimidating competition cars ever built. The 4.5-liter Lampredi V-12 had 340 horsepower which made the 2,400-pound aluminum-bodied (by Pinin Farina) car a handful for any but the most experienced racing drivers. It was the precursor of the 250 MM and competed mostly in long-distance races such as Le Mans and the Carrera Panamericana. Author photos.

The Michelotti/Vignale combination sometimes produced magnificent shapes, but many times they were over-adorned. This 212 Europa, number 0271EU, is a case in point. Brought into the U.S. in 1954 by Alfred Ducato, it has remained in original form and looks the same today as it did when new. Ralph Poole photo.

Similar to the 166 MM was the 212 Export. The bodywork by Carrozzeria Touring was similar but differences can be seen around the grille and tail-light areas, and there was a two-inch difference in wheelbase—the 212 being longer at 88.6 inches. The car shown is number 0158ED. Author photos.

One of Michelotti's most interesting designs was built by Vignale on the Ferrari 340 AT (for America Tubolare) chassis. Three coupes (0222AT, 0224AT and 0226AT) and one roadster (0228AT) were built for the 1952 Carrera Panamericana. The car shown, 0224AT, was driven by Luigi Chinetti to third place behind the Mercedes-Benzes of Kling and Lang. The Ferrari Mexico, as it was called, was at home on long straight stretches of road where top speed could be utilized, but was ill-at-ease on tight, winding roads because of the long wheelbase (102.3 inches) and narrow track (fifty inches). The vertical metal protrusion at the front of each door is a blac device (for boundry layer air control) which was supposed to channel air into the rear fender opening to cool the rear brakes. As things worked out, it was more decorative than functional. Author photos.

✦✦✦✦

Carrozzeria Touring stretched the design of the barchetta to fit the 340 America chassis with a 98.5-inch wheelbase. This car, shown with Jack McAfee winning the Palm Springs main event in March 1953, has the long-block Lampredi V-12 engine. Author photo.

✦✦✦✦✦

Racing and road versions of the 375 MM *berlinetta competizione.* The bumperless car is of the type driven by Maglioli in the 1953 Carrera Panamericana. Pininfarina photos.

Probably one of Vignale's best was this 250 MM roadster, number 0260MM, which was Phil Hill's second Ferrari. Phil won Pebble Beach with the car in 1953, was second at Stead Air Force Base, near Reno, won Santa Barbara, but didn't finish at Moffett Field and Golden Gate Park where in both cases the rear axle failed. Chesebrough photo.

Another rare one; a 166 MM with Vignale body featuring twin windscreens. This car, number 0342M, was brought into the U.S. by screen-writer Ranald MacDougall. It is one of the few 166 V-12's with three four-throat Webers—most had two-throat carbs. Randy had rebodied the 166, wrecked it at Willow Springs in 1954, reinstalled the original body and sold the car. Here it is driven by Jack Brumby at Torrey Pines. Author photo.

A 250 MM (Mille Miglia) berlinetta was the competition car to own in 1953-54. The three-liter V-12 engine was of Colombo origin, but had the individual intake ports and roller cam followers of the Lampredi design, and three four-throat Webers. The bodies were by Pinin Farina and all-aluminum. The car shown, number 0340MM, had more than 100,000 road miles on it when sold by Roger Ellis in 1974. Author photos.

The 375 Mille Miglia shown (0460AM) was purchased new from the factory by Mrs. Robert Day,
in 1954, and has never been raced, even though
the model was created as an all-out competition
car. When Ferrari found out Mrs. Day wanted to
drive the car on the street, he ordered it painted
yellow, and installed green leather upholstery. She
not only kept it that way, but still owns the car.
Author photos.

★★★★★

This is the 250 TR, or Testa Rossa (red head), with a three-liter V-12 single-overhead-camshaft Colombo-designed engine. The car shown (0756) is a 1958 version with 'pontoon' fenders. Later models had smoother body sides, without the protruding nose. The 250 TR was Ferrari's top competition car from 1957 to 1961. Author photos.

A very rare car, the 412 MI, serial number 0744MI, is a "hot rod" assembled for the California Ferrari distributor, John von Neumann, in 1958. It combined the chassis of a 250 TR, with the four-cam V-12 engine from a 335 Sport, which had been originally built for the 1957 Mille Miglia. In 1958, the engine had been installed in a single-seat GT chassis for the 500-mile race at Monza, Italy (the MI stands for Monza/Indianapolis). Author photos.

The Dino 196 S looks like a Testa Rossa and is, in fact, the same basic car with a shortened wheelbase (88.6 instead of 92.5 inches) and a V-6 engine. Some bodies were by Scáglietti, but this car, number 0776TR, has a body by Fantuzzi. The engine is a two-liter, six-cylinder version of the V-12 TR Colombo-designed unit. Geoff Goddard photos.

This is probably the most coveted Ferrari of all, the 250 GTO. The model was first shown at Ferrari's press conference in February 1962, and the first car (3223) had no ducktail spoiler on the back. Subsequent cars had a spoiler built into the body, which was built by Scaglietti to a factory design. The GTO has performance, from its 295 bhp V-12 and five-speed gearbox, and handsome lines. It is the best possible combination of a road/racing car yet built. Thirty-nine 250 GTO's were built in 1962, 1963 and 1964, and they are all accounted for. Look in Jess Pourret's book *The Ferrari Legend: 250 GT Competition,* but don't expect to find one for less than $150,000 in *any* condition—if you can find an owner who will part with it. The car pictured is number 4293. Author photos.

The 330 LMB (Le Mans Berlinetta) was introduced in March 1963 as a competition car to replace the 250 GTO, and was the last front-engined GT car built for competition (the 275 and 365 GTB's were raced, but were built as road cars). The 330 shown is number 4831. Kurt Miska photo.

A 250 LMB (4713) was built, using a 330 body but with a shorter wheelbase—94.5 and 98.4 inches. The main distinguishing feature is the more pronounced ducktail on the 250. Kurt Miska photo.

In November 1963, the 250 LM (for Le Mans) was shown at the Paris Salon, and was the first mid-engined GT car from Ferrari that could be driven on the street with any degree, albeit marginal, of comfort. It has a V-12 engine like that of the Testa Rossa, but with 3.3 liters instead of 3.0; as all 250 LM's after the prototype had the larger engine. Ferrari chose to continue calling the model the 250 because he was seeking homologation for GT racing. The Car shown is number 6107. Author photos.

✪✪✪✪✪

Three of these GTO 64's were built. They are
basically the same as the fastback berlinetta GTO
except for appearance. This is number 5575, the
last GTO built. This body design was a great in-
fluence on GM designers who created the 1968
Corvette, and it's easy to see why. The lines are
functional (other than vision to the rear) and exciting. The car is exceptionally enjoyable to drive, and
the investment has to be one of the best. Kurt
Miska photos.

SERIAL NUMBERS AND
NUMBERING SYSTEM

The first Ferrari sports cars were given three-digit serial numbers with the suffix "C" (for Corsa). It was later replaced by "I" (for Inter), when "C" became a designation for the Grand Prix cars and stood for Competizione. At that point, 1948-49, all competition Ferraris had even-numbered designations, and the street/road cars had odd serial numbers. This continued until the 312, in the mid-sixties, when all Ferraris had odd serial numbers. The Dinos, from the 206 through the 308 GT4, were issued even serial numbers. With the advent of the 308 GTB, all Ferraris, Dino V-8, V-12 or flat-12, were given odd numbers.

When the 166 barchetta was introduced in 1949 (a 166 Mille Miglia with body by Carrozzeria Touring—barchetta meaning "little boat" in Italian), four-digit numbers became the norm, with chassis and engine two numbers apart. This continued through the first twenty-five cars. All the barchettas had even numbers, and early street machines carried three-digit numbers until car number 0051-S which was the first road car with a four-digit number.

Early Ferraris, with Colombo 'short' engines, were designated with the following suffixes:
MM = Mille Miglia, 166 or 250
E = Export, 212
EL = Export Lungo, 195
ED or ET = Export Tubolare
S = Sport, 195
I = Inter, 195
EU = Europa
GT = Grand Touring
C = Corsa

Ferraris with the long-block Lampredi engines carried these suffixes:
AM = America, 340 or 342
AL = America, long chassis
AT = America Tubolare, 340
EU = 250 Europa, long chassis
SA = Superamerica, 400, 410 & 500 Superfast

Confusion is rampant when researching Ferraris because the factory seems to have used both Export and Sport for competition 212's, and the 212 Inter was sometimes called a Europa. Further, serial numbers can't be relied on to establish chronology in the early years. Numbers seem to have been allotted to chassis types, and often cars built months apart will have sequential serial numbers.

Also, even numbers, usually reserved for competition cars, sometimes appeared on road cars. Two such examples are the 340 America (0456AM) built by Pinin Farina for Ingrid Bergman in 1954, and 375 MM (0402AM) built by Scaglietti for Roberto Rossellini in 1955. It is also possible (probable?) that these were competition car chassis diverted to road use, or may even have been rebodied competition cars.

Another factor could be the games Ferrari had to play with the FIA when he was seeking homologation for a new series of Ferraris. The GTO's, for example, which were built in 1963 and 1964, were homologated as Grand Touring cars and all carry odd serial numbers, yet the type is essentially a racing car with a roof.

The normal location of a Ferrari serial number is on the upper side of the left frame tube, near the front exhaust header pipe. This number should match the number stamped on the identification plate attached to the firewall. The engine number is stamped into the cylinder block on the right side at the back.

Sometimes the chassis number has been covered over, particularly if the frame has been reworked or repainted. If your Ferrari is to be a driver and will be strictly for your own enjoyment, the serial number probably isn't terribly important. But, if you're buying the car as an investment, or for show, or if it is a car that is supposed to have a 'history,' make sure you find those serial numbers. They will be important for the documentation of the car, and for future sale.

The short-wheelbase 250 Spyder California—a Ferrari classic! Clive Clark photo.

MODEL DESIGNATION

The first Ferraris, in 1947, were designated by a numbering system based on the capacity, in cubic centimeters, of one cylinder of the engine. These first Ferraris were called 125's—V-12's with 125 cc per cylinder for a total of 1,500 cubic centimeters displacement.

The number designations are rounded off to the next highest whole number; for example, a Ferrari 125 actually has 124.7 cc per cylinder, a 250 has 246.1 and a 500 Mondial has 496.2 cc. Thus, the designations are an "accurate approximation."

The first Dino, the 206, started a new system of number designations, combining displacement in liters and number of cylinders. A 206 had 2.0 liters displacement and six cylinders. A 246 Dino had 2.4 liters displacement and six cylinders. Both cars had V-type engines but, like other Ferrari systems, there is no clue to engine configuration; only size or number of cylinders. The Dino series continues this system through the 308 GT4, GTB and GTS, while the V-12's maintain the original cylinder capacity designation.

Some Examples

125 Corsa, Sport	1500 cc V-12 ($124.7 \times 12 = 1496.4$)
166 Spyder, Mille Miglia	2000 cc V-12
195 Inter, Sport	2300 cc V-12
212 Export, Inter	2600 cc V-12
250 MM, Europa, GTO, TR	3000 cc V-12 ($246.1 \times 12 = 2953.2$)
500 Mondial, Testa Rossa	2000 cc Four
750 Monza	3000 cc Four
860 Monza	3500 cc Four
330 GTC, GTS, P 3/4	4000 cc V-12
340 America, Mexico	4100 cc V-12

Dinos

206 Dino	2.0 liter, V-6
246 Dino	2.4 liter, V-6
248 Dino	2.4 liter, V-8
308 Dino	3.0 liter, V-8

Note: The 400 Superamerica and 500 Superfast don't follow either system. It could be argued that the 400 and 500 numbers are the displacement in deciliters, but this doesn't work for the 410 SA, which has the same displacement as the 500 Superfast and uses the older displacement-per-cylinder system. Also, the 118 and 121 LM's of the mid-fifties follow no known numbering system and it is thought these were internal Ferrari work numbers. It is this sort of thing that makes Ferrari research so frustrating.

FERRARI CLUBS

Ferrari Club of America
Karl Dedolph
200 Webber Hills Rd.
Wayzata, MN 44391
     Membership initiation fee is $10.00 and annual dues are $30.00. Members receive monthly newsletter and quarterly magazine. Club holds at least two national events and many local meets each year.

Ferrari Owners Club
Ed Niles
15910 Ventura Blvd.
Encino, CA 91436
     Membership initiation fee is $10.00 and annual dues are $35.00. Members receive monthly newsletter and quarterly magazine. It is not necessary to own a Ferrari to join. Club holds many events in southwestern U.S.

Ferrari Owners Club (Great Britain)
Godfrey Eaton
10 Whittox Lane
Frome, Somerset
England
Write for information.

The 250 GT berlinetta Lusso is now considered one of the most desirable Ferraris. Pininfarina photo.

Australian Ferrari Register
Barney Govan-Smith
PO Box 203
Shepparton
Victoria 3630
Australia
Write for information.

Club Ferrari NZ
Maurice Paton
16 Toledo Place
Christchurch 8
New Zealand
Write for information.

Southern Equatorial Ferrari Automobili Club
Giorgio E Cavalieri
PO Box 7198, Johannesburg 2000
Republic of South Africa
Write for information.

Club Ferrari France
Pierre Coquet
109 Rue Aristide Briand
92300 Levallois-Perret
France
Write for information.

Ferrari Club Belgio
Pierre Hens
Garage Francorchamps
43-45 Rue Goffart, 1050 Bruxelles
Belgium
Write for information.

Ferraristi Svezia
Rein Tomson
Tvarskedet 26
S-415 06 Gothenburg
Sweden
Write for information.

Ferrari Club Suisse
Jacques Weber
210 route de Meyrin
CH-1217 Meyrin/GE
Switzerland
Write for information.

Ferrari Owners' Club Switzerland
Maurice Labhardt
PO Box 1711, CH-4001 Basle
Switzerland
Write for information.

Ferrari Dino Owners Club
Joachim Alpers
Bruggacherstrasse 12
CH-8617 Monchaltorf
Switzerland
Write for information.

Ferrari Club Drutschland e.V.
Kaiserstrasse 1
D-6600 Saarbrucken
West Germany
Write for information.

Ferrari Club Valenza
Sergio Cassano
Via S. Salvatore 21
15048 Valenza (AL)
Italy
Write for information.

Ferrari Club Japan
T. Kirikae
c/o Racing Service Dino
8-8 Ohmachi, Tsuchiura 300
Japan
Write for information.

FERRARI PRICES 1976-1980

Source: *Ferrari Market Letter,* Vol. 6, No. 2, January 24, 1981.

     Gerald Roush, publisher of the *Ferrari Market Letter,* updates and publishes his price list semi-annually—which is one of the best reasons I can think of for subscribing.

     Prices are based on *asking* prices in his market letter and in other published ads for Ferraris—the cars may or may not have sold for that price. Generally, the quoted prices are a bit higher than actual sale prices.

     Roush has eliminated both the super pristine, squeaky-clean show-only and tacky needs-everything cars. The majority of cars represented by these prices could be purchased and driven with a minimum of work or expense by the new owner.

     No distinctions are made within a type (for example, 275 GTB figures include long- and short-nose, three- and six-carb, steel- and aluminum-body models), nor are years of manufacture considered within a type (with the exception of the 250 GT PF cabriolets which are all Series II cars).

     No similar *asking* price guide is available for the British or European markets, and it's not always pertinent simply to convert American dollars into, say, pounds sterling at the then-appropriate exchange rate. Some models are 'valued' more highly in one market than they are in another.

250 GT PF cabriolet

	High	Avg.	Low
1976	14,750	9,058	5,500
1977	18,000	12,280	7,800
1978	19,000	14,042	7,400
1979	24,500	18,707	14,500
1980	26,000	22,614	18,800

250 GT berlin. Lusso

	High	Avg.	Low
1976	17,500	11,632	8,200
1977	20,000	15,771	7,900
1978	25,000	20,147	11,500
1979	32,000	22,460	18,000
1980	32,500	26,121	16,500

275 GTS

	High	Avg.	Low
1976	25,000	14,639	8,500
1977	29,000	18,783	10,000
1978	32,500	24,675	20,000
1979	32,500	28,982	25,000
1980	37,500	30,873	25,000

250 GT PF coupe

	High	Avg.	Low
1976	12,500	7,255	4,650
1977	15,000	7,740	4,777
1978	16,500	10,134	5,000
1979	16,000	11,005	7,000
1980	19,500	13,891	8,000

330 GT 2+2

	High	Avg.	Low
1976	11,500	8,125	4,300
1977	14,000	8,725	5,000
1978	16,000	10,254	6,200
1979	16,000	11,868	5,500
1980	16,500	12,095	5,995

330 GTC

	High	Avg.	Low
1976	14,900	11,270	8,000
1977	21,000	14,005	8,995
1978	24,500	18,100	10,500
1979	29,500	22,771	17,500
1980	30,000	23,895	16,900

250 GTE 2+2

	High	Avg.	Low
1976	12,000	5,987	4,000
1977	12,500	6,894	4,650
1978	16,900	9,409	5,700
1979	17,000	10,406	5,000
1980	15,000	9,964	7,600

275 GTB

	High	Avg.	Low
1976	17,500	13,973	8,500
1977	26,500	22,125	12,000
1978	32,500	24,911	9,500
1979	39,000	29,743	19,500
1980	49,500	32,297	25,000

330 GTS

	High	Avg.	Low
1976	17,500	15,345	13,500
1977	28,000	23,375	15,000
1978	37,000	29,722	23,000
1979	44,900	35,113	29,500
1980	55,000	46,036	35,000

275 GTB/4

	High	Avg.	Low
1976	25,000	17,940	13,500
1977	32,500	25,987	18,500
1978	37,500	30,089	23,800
1979	45,000	37,032	26,000
1980	51,000	44,556	35,000

365 GTB/4 Spyder

	High	Avg.	Low
1976	45,000	34,115	24,999
1977	90,000	57,831	35,000
1978	100,000	70,435	55,000
1979	125,000	90,605	64,500
1980	150,000	109,336	85,000

Dino 206 GT

	High	Avg.	Low
1976	18,000	14,333	11,500
1977	16,500	13,593	11,900
1978	17,000	15,256	12,500
1979	17,900	16,271	14,500
1980	23,500	18,780	16,500

365 GT 2+2

	High	Avg.	Low
1976	21,500	12,579	8,500
1977	25,000	14,520	11,000
1978	21,000	16,768	11,000
1979	25,500	18,337	12,000
1980	27,000	19,338	13,500

365 GTC/4

	High	Avg.	Low
1976	35,000	24,105	17,800
1977	32,500	25,360	19,000
1978	37,500	28,626	24,500
1979	48,000	33,017	22,000
1980	49,000	35,415	25,000

Dino 246 GT

	High	Avg.	Low
1976	21,000	14,670	9,900
1977	24,000	15,895	10,800
1978	30,000	17,257	12,500
1979	29,000	17,942	11,000
1980	28,500	19,280	12,500

365 GTB/4

	High	Avg.	Low
1976	35,000	23,136	15,000
1977	39,500	26,363	17,500
1978	50,000	33,760	22,000
1979	68,000	40,685	30,000
1980	85,000	52,815	34,900

365 GT4 BB

	High	Avg.	Low
1976	—N/A—		
1977	75,000	59,167	50,000
1978	78,000	54,808	39,000
1979	70,000	59,931	50,000
1980	65,000	58,536	43,000

Dino 246 GTS

	High	Avg.	Low
1976	26,000	19,895	13,500
1977	32,500	21,826	15,500
1978	35,000	23,891	17,500
1979	39,500	26,618	19,500
1980	40,000	28,609	19,500

AUTHORIZED FERRARI DEALERS
North America

ARIZONA
Grand Touring Cars
15115 N. Airport Drive
Scottsdale, AZ 85260
602-991-5320

CALIFORNIA
California Ferrari
1701 Van Ness Avenue
San Francisco, CA 94109
415-771-4070

Ferrari of Los Gatos
66 Main Street
Los Gatos, CA 95030
408-354-4000

Ferrari West Monterey
851 Del Monte Blvd.
Monterey, CA 93940
408-646-3466

Griswold Company
1809 San Pablo Avenue
Berkeley, CA 94702
415-527-5818

R.A.B. Motors
595 Francisco Blvd.
San Rafael, CA 94901
415-454-0582

Wes Lasher, Inc.
5830 Florin Road
Sacramento, CA 95823
916-392-1400

Gardner-Goldman Imports
5787 North Blackstone
Fresno, CA 93710
209-431-7500

Trans World Motors
6290 Hollister Avenue
Goleta, CA 93017
805-964-8774

Ogner Porsche Audi
21301 Ventura Blvd.
Woodland Hills, CA 91364
213-884-4411

Hollywood Sport Cars
5766 Hollywood Blvd.
Hollywood, CA 90028
213-464-6161

Newport Sport Cars
3100 West Coast Highway
Newport Beach, CA 92660
714-642-9405

Mesa Porsche Audi
8333 Hercules Street
La Mesa, CA 92401
714-461-3100

Ferrari of San Diego
500 West "A" Street
San Diego, CA 92110
714-223-2000

Diagnosis Service & Sales
3134 Santa Monica Blvd.
Santa Monica, CA 90404
213-393-9466

CONNECTICUT
Chinetti International Motors
342 W. Putnam Avenue
Greenwich, CT 06830
203-869-9210

FLORIDA
Cressman/Baumgarten Foreign
Cars
615 N. Andrews Avenue
P.O. Box 22878
Ft. Lauderdale, FL 33311
305-523-0907

Cabriolet Ferrari
3780 Bird Road
Miami, FL 33146
305-446-5831

GEORGIA
F.A.F. Motorcars, Inc.
3862 Stephens Court
Tucker, GA 30084
404-939-5464

HAWAII
Love-Thomas Motors
1341 Kapiolani Blvd.
Honolulu, HI 96814
808-521-4771

ILLINOIS
Continental Motors, Inc.
5750 S. LaGrange Road
Countryside, IL 60525
312-352-9200

MASSACHUSETTS
Atlantic Imported Cars, Ltd.
78-88 Prospect Street
Cambridge, MA 02139
617-491-6160

Autohaus, Inc.
742 Cushing Highway
Cohasset, MA 02025
617-383-0095

MICHIGAN
The Sports Car Exchange
14510 Michigan Avenue
Dearborn, MI
313-581-6222

MISSISSIPPI
International Motorcars Corp.
419 S. Gallatin St.
P.O. Box 2441
Jackson, MS 39203
601-969-5668

NEVADA
Modern Classic Motors
3225 Mill Street
Reno, NV 89510
702-323-4160

NEW YORK
Grand Prix SSR Company
36 Route 25A
E. Setauket, NY 11733
516-751-8700

Wide World of Cars
505 East 72 Street
New York, NY 10021
212-535-2200

Wide World of Cars
East Route 59
Spring Valley, NY 10977
914-425-2600

OKLAHOMA
Ralph L. Bolen Imports
1117 N. Robinson
Oklahoma City, OK 73103
405-235-1115

OREGON
Ron Tonkin Gran Turismo
426 N.E. 102nd Avenue
Portland, OR 97220
503-255-4100

PENNSYLVANIA
Algar Enterprises, Inc.
1100 W. Swedesford Road
P.O. Box 455
Paoli, PA 19301
215-647-6660

TEXAS
Bavarian Motors
500 N. Central Expressway
Richardson, TX 75080
214-235-1261

Ferrari of Houston
6541 Southwest Freeway
Houston, TX 77074
713-772-3868

VIRGINIA
Heishman Ferrari
3100 Jefferson Davis Highway
Arlington, VA 22202
703-684-6660

WASHINGTON
Grand Prix Motors
1401 Twelfth Avenue
Seattle, WA 98122
206-329-7070

CANADA
Clarke Simpkins Ltd.
2422 Burrad Street
Vancouver, British Columbia
VJ6 3J4 Canada
604-736-3771

Devonian Motors
11350 Jasper Avenue
Edmonton, Alberta T5K 0L8
Canada
403-426-2616

Luigi Sports Car Sales & Service
4428 St. Catherine St. West
Montreal, Westmount 215
H3Z 1R2 Quebec, Canada
514-937-3763

United Kingdom

CHANNEL ISLANDS
Melbourne Garage Ltd.
Routes des Issues
St. John
Jersey
0534 62709

DEVON
Wadham Stringer (Torquay) Ltd.*
Lisburne Square
Torquay
0803 24321

DORSET
Emblem Sports Cars (UK)*
Pimperne Garage
Blandford
0258 51211

ESSEX
Lancaster Garages Ltd.
Auto Way
Ipswich Road
Colchester
0206 48141

LANCASHIRE
Delamere Motors (Manchester) Ltd.
27 Peter Street
Manchester
061 832 9768

LEICESTERSHIRE
Graypaul Motors Ltd.
Halstead Road
Mountsorrel
Loughborough
0533 374051

LONDON
H.R. Owen Ltd.
2 Lyttleton Road
Hampstead
London N2
01-458 7111

Melton Court
South Kensington
London SW7
01 584 8451

17 Berkeley Street
London W1
01-629 9060

MIDDLESEX
H. R. Owen Ltd.
Western Avenue
Greenford
01-998 7691

NORTHERN IRELAND
Bavarian Garages (NI) Ltd.
17 Bedford Street
Belfast
0232 33331
29 Packenham Street
Belfast
0232 44725

SCOTLAND
J. Colin Briggs Specialist Cars Ltd.
Queenswell Road
Forfar
Angus
0307 64911

Ritchies
393 Shields Road
Glasgow
041-429-5611

SURREY
Maranello Concessionaires Ltd.
Egham By-pass
Egham
0784 36431
Industrial Estate*
Ten Acre Lane
Thorpe
Egham
0784 36222

SUSSEX
Modena Engineering Ltd.
Plummers Plain Garage
nr Handcross
04037 6244

TYNE & WEAR
Reg Vardy Ltd.
The Car Centre
Houghton-le-Spring
Sunderland
0783 842842

WARWICKSHIRE
Brandon Motors Ltd.*
Rugby Road
Brandon
nr Coventry
020354 2285

WEST MIDLANDS
Colmore Depot Ltd.
PO Box 8
22 Hill Street
Birmingham
021 643 337718

*Indicates service or coachwork repair only.

OTHER DEALERS, PARTS AND SERVICE SOURCES

North America

ARIZONA

Paul Johnson Jewelers
1940 E. Camelback
Phoenix, AZ 85106
602-277-1421
jewelry

CALIFORNIA

Bill Rudd Motors
14326 Oxnard Street
Van Nuys, CA 91401
213-788-7833
service, parts, restoration

Borrani Wire Wheel Service
328 Lincoln Blvd.
Venice, CA 90291
213-399-9492
wheel service

Beverly Hills Car Company
9134 Wilshire Blvd.
Beverly Hills, CA 90212
213-276-6149
sales

Dino Enterprises
1341 17th Avenue
San Francisco, CA 94122
415-566-4608
U.S. legal conversions

Automotive Compliance, Inc.
25518 Frampton Avenue
Harbor City, CA 90710
213-539-4880
U.S. legal conversions

R. Straman Co.
779 W. 16th Street
Costa Mesa, CA 92627
714-548-6611
custom bodywork, convertible conversions

Luiz Ferraria Ferrari
755 W. 17th Street, Unit F
Costa Mesa, CA 92627
714-631-3710
service

The Toy Store
11031 Santa Monica Blvd.
Los Angeles, CA 90025
213-473-0847
sales

Preferred Leasing
4790 Convoy Street
San Diego, CA 92111
714-565-9087
car leasing

Zweiful & Associates, Inc.
2901 "B" S. Main Street
Santa Ana, CA 92707
714-549-2147
restoration

Beverly Hills Motoring Accessories
202 S. Robertson
Beverly Hills, CA 90211
213-657-4800
accessories

Waterfront Automobili
Pier 9
San Francisco, CA
415-788-4443
service

Ernie Mendicki
10290 Imperial Ave.
Monta Vista, CA 95014
408-253-6270
Appraisals, consultant

Ed Niles
15910 Ventura Blvd., Suite 1201
Encino, CA 91436
213-986-5030
Appraisals, consultant

Claudio's Italia Sportscars, Inc.
7819 Sepulveda Blvd.
Van Nuys, CA 91405
213-782-6033
service, sales, restoration

Motor Cars of Beverly Hills
8850 Wilshire Blvd.
Beverly Hills, CA 90211
213-659-2300
sales, service

Contemporary Classics Co.
177 F Riverside Avenue
Newport Beach, CA 92663
714-898-6954
accessories, exhaust systems

Goldberg Assoc. International
1323 Lincoln Blvd., Suite 206
Santa Monica, CA 90401
213-451-9243
agents, consultants

USA Conversions
1341 17th Avenue
San Francisco, CA 94122
415-566-4608
U.S. legal conversions

Maranello Motors
5776 Paradise Drive
Corte Madera, CA 94925
415-924-6570
service

Modena Sports Cars
1074 N. Ardmore Ave.
Hollywood, CA 90029
213-660-4960
service

Lyle Tanner Enterprises
10838 Washington Blvd.
Culver City, CA 90230
213-204-5935
parts, accessories

European Auto Restoration
1665 Babcock
Costa Mesa, CA 92627
714-642-0054
restoration, convertible conversions

CONNECTICUT

Amerispec
86 Mill Plain Road
Ridgefield, CT 06877
203-744-0844
U.S. legal conversions

FLORIDA

Faza
2538 S. Ridgewood Ave.
Daytona, FL 32019
904-767-1444
exhaust systems

GEORGIA

Bayless Racing, Inc.
1377 Barclay Circle
Atlanta (Marietta) GA 30060
404-422-6274
Weber carburetor sales, service

ILLINOIS

International Auto, Ltd.
519 N. Milwaukee Avenue
Chicago, IL 60622
312-421-5301
sales

Motorkraft Ltd.
16 W. 281 Thorndale Rd.
Bensenville, IL 60106
312-766-1946
restoration, service

MISSOURI

Archway Motor Imports, Inc.
610 Manchester Road
Manchester (St. Louis) MO 63011
314-227-8303
sales, service, parts

NEW JERSEY

Bremen Automotive, Ltd.
1056 Route 23
North Wayne, NJ
201-696-6060
sales

The Checkered Flag
Millville, NJ
609-696-0110
sales

NEW YORK

Steven Kessler Motor Cars, Inc.
317 E. 34th Street
New York, NY 10016
212-689-0770
sales, service

Concours International Motors
671 Glen Cove Ave.
Glen Head, NY
516-676-2050
sales, service

Louis K. Meisel Gallery
141 Prince Street
New York, NY 10012
212-677-1340
Ferrari prancing horse bronze sculpture

Longford Leasing
113-14 72nd Road
Forrest Hills, NY 11356
212-520-0436
car leasing

Conti Enterprises Corp.
20-23 119th Street
College Point, NY 11356
212-358-1541
exhaust systems

Vintage Car Store, Inc.
93-95 S. Broadway
Nyack, NY 10960
914-358-3800
sales

Maxa Jewelry
34 Cantitoe Road
Yonkers, NY 10710
jewelry

Mark Wallach Ltd.
27 New Street
Nyack-on-the-Hudson, NY 10960
914-358-8179
accessories

Stan Nowak
Box 808
Stony Brook, NY 11790
516-751-1266
auto investment consultant

NORTH CAROLINA

Foreign Cars Italia, Inc.
4100 W. Wendover Avenue
Greensboro, NC 27407
919-852-2158

PENNSYLVANIA

Sinclair's Auto Miniatures, Inc.
3831 W. 12th Street
Erie, PA 16505
814-838-2274
model cars

WISCONSIN

Classic Motorbooks, Inc.
P.O. Box 1
Osceola, WI 54020
715-294-3345
literature

CANADA

Yonge Steeles Motors, Ltd.
7079 Yonge St.
Thornhill, Ontario L3T 2A7
Canada
416-889-2001

United Kingdom

BUCKINGHAMSHIRE

Stratos Developments
1 Yardley Road
Olney
0234 712331
Dino servicing, tuning, special camshafts

Tred-Rite Tyres Ltd.
414 Farnham Road
Slough 0753 30021
wheels, tyres

CHESHIRE

Autobodies Ltd.
16/21 New Zealand Road
Stockpport
061 480 7742
bodywork

ESSEX

Richardson, Hick & Partners Ltd.
325-331 High Road
Ilford
01-514 3333
insurance

GLOUCESTERSHIRE

Scott Rosso
23-25 Victoria Road
Cirencester
0285 4301
restoration, service, sales

HERTFORDSHIRE

Ferrari Mania
Unit 9, Orchard Road
Royston
0763 45021
bodywork, mechanics

LONDON

Motorstyle Ltd.
12/13 The Arches
Munster Road, SW6
01-731 5703
service

MIDDLESEX

DK Engineering
Whittles Yard
10-16 Hallowell Road
Northwood
09274 21399
service, restoration

NORTHAMPTONSHIRE

Automotive Designs Ltd.
1 Gate Lodge
Round Spinney Indust. Est.
0604 43901
rebuilds, restoration, conversion

GTC Engineering
Unit 5
Sanders Lodge Indust. Est.
Rushden
09334 55396
service, restoration

SURREY

Autocraft Ltd.
Unit 815
Brooklands Indust. Park
Weybridge
0932 56642
conversions, restoration

Modena Engineering Ltd.
East Horsley
04865 4663
sales, repairs, restoration

Moto Technique Ltd.
Pycroft Road
Chertsey
09328 64706
restoration, bodywork, refurbishing

Rardley (Motors) Ltd.
Headley Road
Grayshett
042 873 6606
trimming, refurbishing, restoration

John Scott & Partners Ltd.
10 The Borough
Farnham
0252 725555
insurance

WEST MIDLANDS

HBM
Unit 4
Cross Street North
Springfield, Wolverhampton
078571 2056
promotion, rental

Ferrari's first streetable mid-engined GT, the 250 LM; truly an exotic among exotics. Author photo.

RECOMMENDED FERRARI BOOKS

Almost one hundred books have been published about Enzo Ferrari or Ferrari automobiles. Each of them has *something* in it that is interesting, or different from all the other books. Sometimes it is a photo of a car that hasn't been seen by many Ferrari enthusiasts; sometimes it is a different view of a familiar car that seems to always be pictured from the same angle; or maybe it is a bit of information that has previously been ignored or unsubstantiated.

Many of these books are in foreign languages, many are out of print. Some are on a very limited aspect of the Ferrari history. Following is a list of books that I feel are good value for the money (well-researched and as accurate as possible, pertaining to the cars discussed in this book). It is not a complete list of available books, but could be considered a 'starter' list for your Ferrari library.

FERRARI: The Sports & Gran Turismo Cars (fourth revised edition)
Fitzgerald, Merritt & Thompson
W. W. Norton and Company, Inc., Copyright 1979
(copyright 1968 by Bond Publishing, copyright 1976 by CBS Publications)
280 pages, hardcover, ISBN 0-393-01276-X
This book tries to cover all Ferrari sports and grand touring cars built since 1947, and comes close to doing it. It is probably the one book about Ferraris you should buy, if you buy only one book.

FERRARI: The Man, The Machines
Automobile Quarterly, edited by Stan Grayson
E. P. Dutton Company, Inc., Copyright 1975
348 pages, hardcover, ISBN 0-525-10445-3
A compilation of material by journalists and racing drivers. Good all-around history and philosophy of the company and the people who helped make Ferraris famous.

THE FERRARI LEGEND: 250 GT Competition
Jess G. Pourret
John W. Barnes, Jr. Publishing, Inc., Copyright 1977
382 pages, hardcover, ISBN 0-914822-11-X
A tremendous research project that details the history of the 250 GT competition berlinettas from the long-wheelbase ''Tour de France'' and short-wheelbase cars through the GTO. History, competition record, specifications.

FERRARI: Brochures and Sales Literature
Richard F. Merritt
John W. Barnes, Jr. Publishing, Inc., Copyright 1976
286 pages, softcover, ISBN 0-914822-05-5
Reprints of all the known brochures and factory sales literature published about the cars built from 1946 to 1967. Useful for determining original specifications. Be wary of weight figures.

FERRARI: The Early Berlinettas & Competition Coupes
Dean Batchelor
db Publications, Copyright 1974
96 pages, softcover, ISBN 0-914792-00-8

   Brief history, competition record and specifications of Ferrari berlinettas from 1947 to 1962. Spec charts are probably the most valuable part of the book.

FERRARI: The Early Spyders & Competition Roadsters.
Dean Batchelor
db Publications, Copyright 1975
128 pages, softcover, ISBN 0-914792-01-6

   Brief history, competition record and specifications of Ferrari spyders from 1947 to 1962. Spec charts are probably the most valuable part of the book.

FERRARI: The Gran Turismo & Competition Berlinettas
Dean Batchelor
db Publications, Copyright 1977
96 pages, softcover, ISBN 0-914792-02-4

   Brief history, competition record and specifications of Ferrari competition berlinettas from 1962 to the 512 BB. Again, the spec charts are most valuable.

THE BERLINETTA LUSSO: A Ferrari of Unusual Elegance
Kurt H. Miska
John W. Barnes, Jr. Publishing, Inc., Copyright 1978
96 pages, softcover, ISBN 0-914822-14-4

   One of the first books devoted entirely to one Ferrari model. Highly recommended for those wanting to learn everything about the Lusso history and specifications.

THE SPYDER CALIFORNIA: A Ferrari of Particular Distinction
George M. Carrick
John W. Barnes, Jr. Publishing, Inc., Copyright 1976
76 pages, softcover, ISBN 0-914822-07-1

   This book covers the long- and short-wheelbase Californias, with some history of the cabriolets. Specifications, competition history and a list of serial numbers.

FERRARI
Hans Tanner & Doug Nye (fifth revised edition)
Haynes Publishing, Copyright 1979
542 pages, hardcover, ISBN 0-85429-2381

   One of the first Ferrari books, now in its fifth edition. *Ferrari* covers all models built by Ferrari up to the date of revision. Contains a surprising amount of information about each model in view of the vast number of models covered.

DINO: The Little Ferrari
Doug Nye
John W. Barnes, Jr. Publishing, Inc., Copyright 1979
328 pages, hardcover, ISBN 0-914822-24-1

Coverage of all Ferraris with the Dino six- or eight-cylinder engines, many of which are Grand Prix or sports racing cars. A must for anyone interested in this model.

THE FERRARI LEGEND: The Road Cars
Antoine Prunet
W. W. Norton, Copyright 1981
446 pages, hardcover, ISBN 0-85059-433-2

A must for any Ferrari enthusiast, covering the road cars from the very first in 1947 through the 512 BB, in text and photos—many never before published. One of the most accurate books published about Ferraris.

FERRARI CARS 1946-1956
FERRARI CARS 1957-1962
FERRARI CARS 1962-1966
FERRARI CARS 1966-1969
FERRARI CARS 1969-1973
R. M. Clarke, Brooklands Books
American distribution by Motorbooks International.
100 pages each, softcover

These are reprints of Ferrari articles, of each period as dated, from U.S., British and European automotive publications. Regular readers of *Road & Track, Car and Driver, Sports Car Graphic, Autocar, Motor, et al,* will probably have read many of these when they were first published. Reproduction is not great, but it is nice to have so many related cars covered in one book.

BOXER: The Ferrari Flat-12 Racing & GT Cars
Johnathan Thompson
Newport Press and Osprey Publishing Ltd., Copyright 1981
184 pages, hardcover, ISBN: 0-930880-05-6 and 0-85045-409-3

Gives full story of every flat-12 racing and GT car ever built from the 1.5-liter 512 F1 in 1964 to the 365 GT/BB512 road cars. The latest word on these models.

FERRARI TESTA ROSSA V-12
Joel E. Finn
Newport Press, Copyright 1979
250 pages, hardcover, ISBN: 0-930880-03-X

Does emminent justice to these 34 cars. Gives excellent source of basic Ferrari information; background, development and racing activity. Will delight every Ferrari enthusiast.

FERRARI BERLINETTA BOXER
Mel Nichols
Osprey Publishing Ltd., Copyright 1979
136 pages, hardcover, ISBN: 0-85045-326-7
 Strong pictorial coverage and high overall quality tell the story of the 365 and 512 series.

FERRARI DINO 206GT, 246GT & GTS
Osprey Publishing, Ltd., Copyright 1980
136 pages, hardcover, ISBN: 0-85045-365-8
 Text and photos highlight the cars, production and racing careers of these fabulous Pininfarina V-6 road cars. Necessary reading for the enthusiast.

FERRARI 275 GTB & GTS
Ian Webb
Osprey Publishing, Ltd., Copyright 1981
136 pages, hardcover, ISBN: 0-85045-4-2-6
 Neatly encapsulates the life and times of these models including the 2-cam, 4-cam, Competizione and Spider. This book should be in the library of every lover of fine exotic automobiles.

THE SCUDERIA FERRARI
Luigi Orsini and Franco Zagari
Osprey Publishing, Ltd., Copyright 1981
400 pages, hardcover, ISBN: 0-85045-378-X
 A remarkable collection of previously unpublished (in the English language) information and photos of an important auto racing decade.

MAGAZINE ARTICLES
ABOUT FERRARIS

Following is a list of magazine articles published in the U.S. in recent years pertaining to the types and models of Ferraris listed in this book. Features about Grand Prix Ferraris or personality bios have not been included. The list is as complete as possible, based on information furnished by the magazines' publishers. In each case, the magazine address is included so you can contact the publisher for copies of a particular issue. If the publisher does not have a complete set of magazines that can be sold, a Xerox copy can, at least, furnish the information needed to help evaluate a particular car.

Similar cars are often covered by different magazines and, in some cases, similar cars are covered several years later by the same magazine. The specifications will vary from report to report, sometimes because the cars changed, but often because the information source for the magazine was not always accurate. And you will find a tremendous difference in expressed opinions about any given vehicle. This is to be expected, and you can only use these reports as guidelines to form your own opinions which, in the long run, are the ones that count.

Road tests and technical features have also been published in British and other magazines. Most British magazines do provide a reprint service and their addresses are provided at the end of this listing.

Autoweek
965 E. Jefferson Ave.
Detroit, MI 48207
313-567-9520

Published weekly

Weekly tabloid covering industry news and competition events. Good classified ad section.

Car and Driver
2002 Hogback Road
Ann Arbor, MI 48104
313-994-0055

Published monthly

Jan 1958	250 GT Europa
Apr 1958	1958 Ferraris
Sept 1958	4.9 Superfast
Sept 1959	250 GT California & berlinetta
Oct 1960	250 GT berlinetta
Jan 1961	250 GT 2+2
April 1963	400 Superamerica
March 1965	330 GT 2+2
May 1965	275 LM
Oct 1965	275 GTS
July 1967	330 GTC
Oct 1967	275 GTB4
Jan 1968	275 GTB4, 330 GTC

Sept 1968	275 GTB4/Maserati/ Aston Martin/Lamborghini
March 1969	365 GT 2+2
Jan 1970	365 GTB4 Daytona
June 1975	308 GT4/Maserati Merak
Nov 1976	365 GT BB
March 1977	308 GTB
July 1977	400 Automatic
June 1978	308 GTS
Dec 1979	308 GT4
June 1980	308 GTS
Oct 1980	308 GTBi

Cavallino
Box 323
Scarsdale, NY 10583
914-472-2852

Published bi-monthly

This is the only magazine devoted entirely to Ferrari cars.

Vol 1, No. 1	225 Sport, and listing of early serial numbers
Vol 1, No. 2	400 A, 250 MM, and early serial numbers
Vol 1, No. 3	ASA 1000
Vol 1, No. 4	Superamerica and Superfast

Vol 1, No. 5   308 GT4
Vol 1, No. 6   Daytona "Spyder conversions"
Vol 2, No. 1   400 SA, Superfast, more early serial numbers
No. 8   250 MM, Competition Boxers
No. 9   2+2's and 275 GTB
No. 10   342 and 375 Americas, 308 GTS

Ferrari Market Letter
Gerald Roush
850 Maxey Hill Court
Stone Mountain, GA 30083
404-292-4162

Published bi-weekly

Has been published for five years. Each letter has one page of editorial comment pertaining to a specific model or style of Ferrari, and the balance is advertising for Ferrari cars and parts. Back issues are available.

Road & Track
1499 Monrovia Ave.
Newport Beach, CA 92663
714-646-4455

Published monthly

June 1960   250 GT PF coupe
Aug 1962   250 GT 2+2
Dec 1962   410 Superamerica
June 1963   400 Superamerica
April 1964   Ferrari Looks at '64
Dec 1964   275 GTB & GTS
Sept 1966   275 GTS
Sept 1967   275 GTS/4 NART Spyder
Aug 1968   330 GTS
Dec 1968   365 GTB4 Daytona
June 1969   250 GT Lusso
Nov 1969   365 GT 2+2
Oct 1970   365 GTB4 Daytona
May 1972   246 GT Dino
July 1972   365 GTC4
Feb 1974   246 GTS/Porsche/ 450 SL/Corvette/XK-E
Nov 1974   Ferrari Daytonas for Road and Race
June 1975   365 GT BB
Sept 1975   308 GT4/Maserati Merak/Lamborghini Urraco
March 1976   308 GTB
Dec 1976   308 GTB
Feb 1977   308 GTB
Mar 1978   512 BB
July 1978   308 GTS
Nov 1979   308 GT4

Sports Car Graphic
8490 Sunset Blvd.
Los Angeles, CA 90069
213-657-5100

Currently published quarterly, was monthly from 1961 to 1970. No subscriptions sold at this time.

June 1960   Ferrari - World's Best
June 1962   Ferrari for 1962
Jan 1963   ASA 1000
May 1963   Ferrari for 1963
Apr 1964   Ferrari for 1964
Aug 1964   330 2+2
July 1965   275 LM
Oct 1965   275 GTB
Jan 1967   330 2+2
Feb 1967   330 GTC
Nov 1968   365 2+2
Mar 1969   206 Dino
No. 1   308 GTB & GTS, 400 A and You *Can* Own a Ferrari
No. 3   308 GTS, 410 SA
No. 4   308 GT4
No. 7   250 LM

Autocar
IPC Transport Press
Quadrant House, The Quadrant
Sutton, Surrey SM2 5AS
01-661 3500

Published weekly

General motoring magazine with good road tests, some features with industry and sports news.

Autosport
Haymarket Publishing Ltd.
38/42 Hampton Road
Teddington, Middx.
01-977 8787

Published weekly

High-quality sports magazine but with road tests and some historical features. Good racing advertisements.

Car
FF Publishing Ltd.
64 West Smithfield
London EC1A 9EE
01-606 7836

Published monthly

English *Car and Driver* doesn't do it justice. Superb features and design. Pro, exotic cars and industry scoops.

Classic and Sports Cars
Haymarket Publishing Ltd.
38/42 Hampton Road
Teddington, Middx.
01-977 8787

Published monthly

As *Classic Car* but with slightly more modern approach. Much more road test material both old and new. Was known as *Old Motor*.

Motor
IPC Transport Press
Surrey House, 1 Throwley Way
Sutton, Surrey SM1 4QQ
01-643 8040

Published weekly

As *Autocar* but usually with more features.

Motor Sport
Standard House, Bonhill Street
London EC2A 4DA
01-628 4741

Published monthly

Traditional magazine with competition and feature coverage. Excellent classified ad section.

Motoring News
Standard House, Bonhill Street
London EC2A 4DA
01-628 4741

Published weekly

Tabloid newspaper covering industry but concentrating on competition events.

Thoroughbred and Classic Cars
IPC Transport Press
Quadrant House, The Quadrant
Sutton, Surrey SM2 5AS
01-661 3500

Published monthly

Feature magazine with good classified advertising; combines old and new.

MORE GREAT READING

Illustrated Porsche Buyer's Guide. Covers the 356 through the 944 from 1950 to 1983 with lots of photos. Softbound, 175 pages.

Illustrated Corvette Buyer's Guide. Includes 194 photos and lots of info on all these cars 1953-1982. 156 pages, softbound.

Illustrated High Performance Mustang Buyer's Guide. Covers the 1965 GT, the Shelby, through the 1973 Mach 1. Softbound, 250 illustrations, 176 pages.

Illustrated Alfa Romeo Buyer's Guide. The 6C-2500 through the Montreal are covered with over 200 illustrations. 176 pages, softbound.

The Big Healeys: A Collector's Guide, by Graham Robson. 128 pages, 130 illustrations.

Classic Jaguar Saloons: A Collector's Guide, by Chris Harvey. 128 pages, 135 illustrations.

The Jaguar E-Type: A Collector's Guide, by Paul Skilleter. 128 pages, 160 illustrations.

The Jaguar XK: A Collector's Guide, by Paul Skilleter. 128 pages, 140 illustrations.

The Lotus Elan and Europa: A Collector's Guide, by john Bolster. 126 pages, 135 illustrations.

MG: The Art of Abingdon, by John McLellan. Lavish pictorial history of Britain's famous sports car and its factory. 256 pages, 480 illustrations.

The MGA, MGB & MGC: A Collector's Guide, by Graham Robson. 136 pages, 146 illustrations.

The Porsche 911: A Collector's Guide, by Michael Cotton. 128 pages, 140 illustrations.

The Sprites & Midgets: A Collector's Guide, by Eric Dymock. 128 pages, 130 illustrations.

The T-Series MG: A Collector's Guide, by Graham Robson. 128 pages, 131 illustrations.

The Triumph TRs: A Collector's Guide, by Graham Robson. 150 pages, 200 illustrations.

The Z-Series Datsuns: A Collector's Guide, by Ray Hutton. 128 pages, 140 illustrations.

The Story of Lotus: 1947–1960, Birth of a Legend, By Ian H. Smith. 192 pages, 180 illustrations.

The Story of Lotus: 1961–1971, Growth of a Legend, by Doug Nye. 288 pages, 280 illustrations.

Triumph Cars: The Complete 75-Year History, by Richard Langworth and Graham Robson. Over 400 pictures supplement this definitive history along with comprehensive appendices. 312 pages.

The Corvettes 1953–1984: A Collector's Guide, by Richard Langworth. 128 pages, 130 illustrations.

Lamborghini: A Collector's Guide, by Chris Harvey. 128 pages, 127 illustrations.